Philosophy, Religion, and the Meaning of Life
Part III

Professor Francis J. Ambrosio

THE TEACHING COMPANY ®

PUBLISHED BY:

THE TEACHING COMPANY
4840 Westfields Boulevard, Suite 500
Chantilly, Virginia 20151-2299
1-800-TEACH-12
Fax—703-378-3819
www.teach12.com

ISBN 1-59803-582-7

Francis J. Ambrosio

Associate Professor of Philosophy
Georgetown University

Professor Francis J. Ambrosio is Associate Professor of Philosophy at Georgetown University. After studying Italian language and literature in Florence, Italy, he completed his Ph.D. at Fordham University with a specialization in contemporary European philosophy. He has lectured widely in the United States, Germany, and Italy. He currently teaches courses at Georgetown on Plato, existentialism, hermeneutics, and deconstruction and an interdisciplinary course entitled Dante and the Christian Imagination. As a member of the Core Faculty of the Liberal Studies Program at Georgetown, he has regularly taught undergraduate and graduate interdisciplinary courses to adult lifelong learners throughout his career.

Between 1987 and 2005, Professor Ambrosio conducted study programs annually for Georgetown at Villa Le Balze, the university's academic Center in Fiesole, Italy. These courses—which he team taught with his wife and colleague, Deborah Warin, director of the College Credit Evaluation Service at the American Council on Education—focused on the transition in culture from the Middle Ages to the Renaissance, especially in Florence and the cities of Tuscany, Umbria, and Le Marche. In 1997, Professor Ambrosio published a study of the painting of Fra Angelico, entitled *Fra Angelico at San Marco: The Place of Art*.

Professor Ambrosio has written on hermeneutics, especially the work of Hans-Georg Gadamer, in scholarly journals such as *Journal of the British Society for Phenomenology*, *International Philosophical Quarterly*, *Man and World*, *Owl of Minerva*, and *American Catholic Philosophical Quarterly*. He has contributed chapters to several collections, including the Library of Living Philosophers volume on Gadamer. In addition, he is the editor of two books: *Text and Teaching* (Georgetown University Press, 1991) and *The Question of Christian Philosophy Today* (Fordham University Press, 1999). His most recent book, entitled *Dante and Derrida: Face to Face*, was published by The State University of New York Press in 2007.

In 1994, Professor Ambrosio was the convener of a major academic gathering at Georgetown University, entitled "The Question of Christian Philosophy Today: An International Symposium." It attracted over 140 attendees from more than 30 institutions. Subsequently, he edited and published the symposium papers, with an introduction and contributed essay.

In 1998, Professor Ambrosio was the recipient of the Bunn Award for Faculty Excellence, selected by the students of Georgetown University. In 2000, he received the Dean's Award for Teaching from Georgetown University. In 2009, he was awarded the Dorothy Brown Award for Outstanding Teaching Achievement, which is selected by a university-wide vote of Georgetown's undergraduate students.

In 2000, Professor Ambrosio founded the *MyDante* project (http://dante.georgetown.edu) at Georgetown University, which has been widely recognized as one of the most innovative and effective educational websites currently available in the field of humanities. With a fully interactive, web-based edition of Dante's *Commedia* at its heart, the project invites readers to develop their own annotated version of Dante's poem through a rich pedagogy of reading and reflection.

Table of Contents
Philosophy, Religion, and the Meaning of Life
Part III

Philosophy, Religion, and the Meaning of Life

Scope:

The subject matter of this course is unusual and unique. It is not a body of knowledge to be investigated or method of inquiry to be mastered, but rather the dynamic history of a mystery which reveals itself through the power of a question: the question of the meaning of life. In choosing to undertake this kind of subject, the goal cannot be to answer the question, but rather to try to do justice to it by allowing ourselves to experience the full power of the question itself. In other words, we shall endeavor to follow the advice given by Rainer Maria Rilke, the 20th-century Austrian poet, who wrote to a young person seeking guidance:

> I want to urge you as much as I can, dear friend, to be patient toward all that is unsolved in your heart and to try to love the questions themselves like locked rooms and like books that are written in a very foreign tongue. Do not seek to have answers, which cannot be given to you because you would not be able to live them. And the point is to live everything. Live the questions now. Perhaps you will then gradually, without noticing it, live along some distant day into an answer.

Rilke's advice, wise as it might seem to be, is neither original nor unique to him. The question of the meaning of life has a history as long as the history of humankind itself, a history which has left us a rich and diverse "wisdom tradition" upon which we can draw in the form of teachings of many sorts: religious, philosophical, scientific, artistic, moral, political, and practical. But at the same time, this wisdom tradition really does bequeath its heritage as an embarrassment of riches—so many possibilities, all credible and time tested, bright with promise and hope. Yet each is coming at the price of a life and death, an all or nothing with no second chance, because for each person who says "I," the way "I" choose to live my life decides who I am, forever. Or does it? Does anyone ever truly "have" an identity? Is it certain that life does have meaning? A meaning? Many meanings? Paradoxically, must we not ask what the question itself means, and at the same time try to gauge what is at stake in asking this question? Everything? Nothing? How does one measure the horizon?

Situated as we are today, with 5,000 years or so of recorded human history as our immediate horizon, experience has at least begun to teach us to be on the lookout for wisdom's impostors: dogmatic fundamentalism and unyielding totalitarian absolutism of every kind on the one hand; ever shifting, elusive relativism and corrosive skepticism on the other, offering no solid ground on which to take a stand. To ask the question of the meaning of life for ourselves while at the same time also trying to learn from the wisdom of those who have gone before us, demands that we make ourselves at home in the no man's land between the false security of certainty and a casual promiscuity of indifference. To use an economic metaphor: In the marketplace of life wisdom always comes packaged with the disclaimer: *Caveat emptor*! Let the buyer beware!

For this reason, the course we set for ourselves must make its choices and be prepared to deal with their consequences. First, while remaining mindful of the distinctive wisdom tradition of the East, our study will limit itself to examining in detail the history of appropriation of the wisdom of human experience by Western civilization. Recognizing the realistic limits of the time available to us, our course emphasizes the depth of historical analysis over pluralistic breadth of inclusion, without making hastily generalizations, or failing to identify ways in which we can use the boundaries of the path we have chosen to recognize clues for further exploration. Furthermore, our investigation focuses on one particularly central dynamic in Western history: the tension between the wisdom tradition arising from the Greco-Roman culture of secular humanism on the one hand, and the distinctively different legacy of wisdom distilled from the worldview of Judeo-Christian and Islamic theistic religion on the other. Taking the figures of the hero and of the saint as paradigmatic of each of these wisdom traditions respectively, this course examines the path to wisdom traced by each of these exemplary explorers of the question, how do you live a meaningful life? In the simplest terms, putting the question this way: Is meaning to be found in life, if it is to be found at all, by trying to become a hero or a saint? Or, perhaps more modestly, is it to be found by at least trying to learn from heroes or from saints? Should I try to fulfill my own potential as a person, to be all that I can be, to be a hero, in other words, or should I live for loving others and give my life as a gift to them? What do I owe myself? What do I owe others? How is it possible, (is it possible?), to weigh and balance both sides of the scale?

To begin, we first sketch out the worldview that opens up for us when we look out through the eyes of each figure: For the hero, reality appears as fundamentally shaped by the human struggle with impersonal forces of necessity and fate that are in the end indifferent to human hopes and fears; for the saint, reality is ultimately configured by the bonds of a covenant relationship among persons, human and divine, based on an exchange of promises offered in the mutual hope of unconditional trust. Put briefly, for the hero the meaning of life is honor; for the saint, it is love. We look to heroes with admiration and respect, seeking inspiration. We turn to saints with gratitude and humility, asking help.

But how are we to think about and discuss the relationship between these two exemplary types, and perhaps more importantly, what are we to do about them in our lives? Are these two paths compatible, and to what extent? Or do they ultimately pose an implacable choice to be made to live either for the sake of the self or for the sake of the other person. The primary task this course sets is a far reaching examination of diverse individuals who, either through their thought or the dedication of their lives, can sharpen our focus on precisely what it requires to be a hero or a saint. Our historical study will make it clear that a deep, quasi-genetic tension exists between the two, so that realistically we might have to lower our expectations of being able to be both a hero and a saint. As our course of study unfolds, the historical evidence would seem to push us progressively to consider the possibility that these two ways of life cannot always be harmoniously integrated in our personal identities, so that at least from time to time, perhaps constantly, we must choose between. But how? Here we discover what will emerge as the focal issue of our questioning: Can the question of the meaning of life be seriously engaged at all without immediately confronting and feeling the full force of the question of the meaning of death as its inseparable companion?

In pursuing this investigation of the hero and the saint, Part One of the course will trace two parallel but distinct genealogical histories of cultural heredity. One line of descent originates in Greek culture with the figure of Socrates, the other line of descent traces from Abraham. In Part Two, we discover in Saint Paul and Saint Augustine the first major attempt to synthesize the two archetypes of hero and saint in the ideal of one unified culture of Christian humanism. But the instability inherent in this genetic hybrid reveals itself in the novel mutations of the type manifested by figures such as the Prophet Mohammed announcing the rise of Islam; the "fool for God" portrayed by Francis of Assisi; the cosmic pilgrim in Dante's Christian epic, the *Divine Comedy*; and the pivotal figure of Michelangelo, the last great exemplar of the Christian humanist ideal and at the same time arguably the first truly modern person. Passing through the radical new beginning envisioned by the Enlightenment, the tension between these two ideal types of human living finally proves too unstable to hold together and culminates in Nietzsche's Zarathustra, who announces the "death of God" and reasserts the purer form of the Greek hero of self-mastery and self-fulfillment.

After considering Kierkegaard and Dostoevsky's alternative responses to this crisis in the Western experiment with the hero-saint, we turn in Part Three to the 20th century's attempt to reformulate the question of the meaning of life in terms of variant mutations of the traditional paradigms, introducing us first to the "anti-hero," appearing in the works of writers like Sartre, Camus, and Beckett; and to the "secular saint" portrayed by Flannery O'Connor, Levinas, and Simone Weil, among others. We conclude with a reflection on the pessimism of Freud regarding the "future of an illusion" and the vision of sober hope sketched by Ernest Becker in his meditation on the finality of death.

Throughout the course, this historical investigation will be punctuated by reference to contemporary thinkers, novels, films, and plays that challenge us to consider the application of both traditional paradigms to the experience of contemporary existence regarding how to go about asking the question of the meaning of life. In the end, we seek to be in a position to validate for ourselves, both intellectually and experientially, that there is indeed more reality and truth in the committed and integral pursuit of the question of the meaning of life than there is in any willful attempt to stem the sweeping tide of historical change and to fix the mysterious reality of existence in the false security of any fixed or exclusive answer to it.

Lecture Twenty-Five
Camus and the Absurd Hero

Scope:

Continuing our study of existentialism as a transformation of the classical humanistic hero ideal into the traumatic context of the 20th century, this lecture considers the unique contribution of Albert Camus to French existentialism. In his first and most unsettling novel, Camus offers a portrait of contemporary human existence in a state of culturally induced alienation and desensitization in his portrayal of *The Stranger*. In the title character Mersault, we catch a glimpse of all that is left of human identity when a person refuses either to affirm or deny the cultural conventions of meaning except as validated in one's own immediate experience. Then, in *The Myth of Sisyphus*, Camus uses the Greek hero who loved life and scorned death to portray an affirmation of personal existence that does not require meaning, but lays claim to dignity and even a kind of happiness through revolt against the absurdity of human condition.

Outline

I. Providing another perspective on existentialism, Albert Camus asserts that the heroic worldview is best characterized as "absurd."

   A. Camus did not consider himself an existentialist.

   B. We will utilize Camus' emphasis on rebellion to focus our attention on what might emerge as the most radical element in heroic identity as a pathway in the human search for meaning.

   C. That most fundamental element for Camus is a willingness to face the question "Could human existence possibly be genuinely and altogether absurd?" and to face it without any of the avenues of escape which society provides; in other words, with the integrity of self-mastery.

II. Albert Camus' life sheds some light on his singular emphasis on "rebellion" as an authentic pathway in the search for meaning.

   A. Throughout his life Camus experienced identity conflict resulting from colonialism, caught between distinct nationalisms, religious sensibilities, and cultural identities.

B. Gifted intellectually, Camus was dependent on scholarships to pursue his education in a climate of uncertainty.

C. Camus was stricken with tuberculosis at age 17; the disease afflicted him throughout his life.

D. His personal relationships were troubled and unstable through two marriages and several intense affairs.

E. As a young man he saw communism as a way of contesting colonial oppression, but rejected party orthodoxy and moved toward anarchism, joining the resistance during WWII.

III. In his first novel, *The Stranger*, Camus asks us to imagine living a human life convinced that one's existence were a matter of indifference to the universe.

IV. The novel imagines a hero who is alone although he has a mother, a lover, friends, an enemy, a judge, a priest, and a crowd of witnesses to his execution. The hero goes to his death with a kind of certainty, a kind of happiness, and a kind of fellowship with the witnesses of his execution. He is an absurd hero.

A. Mersault's heroism consists of nothing more than this, but of no less than this either: He refuses to lie, or to do what he does not feel or see the reason for.

B. Mersault enters life disarmed, we do not know why. He lacks the armor of the social conventions and ideologies that characterize "normal living."

C. Mersault is a hero because he does not rely on anyone but himself or on anything that is not his own to avoid facing the possibility that the universe might be genuinely indifferent.

D. The absurdity of existence which Camus portrays is not a claim about reality; it is not a truth claim. Rather the absurdity is the possibility that our attitudes toward reality, our faith in meaning, our solidarity, compassion, and love, even our forgiveness might be simply beside the point, even though it feels as if we could not possibly live without them.

V. In the *Myth of Sisyphus*, Camus imagines another, more mythic version of the absurd hero, again asking: Can one actually imagine living happily without meaning?

    A. The essay asserts that there is really only one philosophically important question: whether to commit suicide.

    B. Camus makes the point that the heroism of the absurd has its *arete* in a quality of lucidity and self-certainty.

Suggested Reading:

Camus, *The Myth of Sisyphus*.

———, *The Plague*.

———, *The Stranger*.

Lottman, *Albert Camus*.

Questions to Consider:

1. Were you surprised by Camus' comment on Saint Francis? Why or why not?

2. How might Camus' portrayal of human existence as absurd relate to Kierkegaard's notion of the "leap of faith"?

Lecture Twenty-Five—Transcript
Camus and the Absurd Hero

In the last lecture, we saw the image of the hero pushed to its extreme limit by Sartre and de Beauvoir in the confrontation with totalitarian violence. It's at this extreme limit of heroic identity that Alfred Camus joins the conversation. Providing another perspective on existentialism, Albert Camus asserts that the heroic worldview is most truthfully and most valuably characterized as the view that reality or the human situation in reality is ultimately, genuinely absurd. Camus can be understood as asking, in other words, whether, in a totally ironic sense, the absurd itself might not be the source of meaning and fulfillment in human existence, and that through the experience to which Camus refers as "rebellion." Camus did not consider himself an existentialist. When he and Sartre became acquainted, they found they had many disagreements, both philosophical and political; and, as we shall see, Camus nevertheless responded creatively to many of the concerns that occupied de Beauvoir and Sartre. Here in this lecture we'll analyze the difference between Sartre and de Beauvoir on the one hand and Camus on the other in terms of Sartre's emphasis on total responsibility, contrasting that with Camus' emphasis on rebellion. Thus we will utilize Camus' emphasis on rebellion to focus our attention on what might emerge as the most radical element in heroic identity as a pathway in the search for meaning in human existence.

That most fundamental human issue for Camus can be articulated as a willingness to face the question: Could human existence possibly be genuinely and altogether absurd; without meaning; without establishing any lasting contact with a reality larger than itself? Could it really be, as Sartre would argue, out of all relationship to anything other than itself in its living and in its dying? Camus wants to take total responsibility for the question of absurdity, and to face it without any of the avenues of what he and the other existentialists would characterize as escape, which society provides. In other words, wants to face it with the integrity of self-mastery and self-possession, with an integrity of personal identity for which he can take full responsibility. We're suggesting that Camus' artistic and philosophical strategy is designed to encourage and support this extreme heroic adventure by demonstrating that it is possible to imagine human existence as absurd without negating the possibility of living a meaningful life or of devaluing the significance of human action. That suggestion, of course, flies in the face of anything that could properly be called rationality; but to dismiss it because it is technically irrational is to beg the question: Is there a source of meaning in human existence that does not depend only on rationality but does not have any foundation at all except the bottomless abyss of human freedom?

As we've seen, once we are able to realistically imagine human existence according to a worldview and a structure of meaning that genuinely differs from the societally acceptable norms, then we're forced to recognize that living according to the meaning and values embraced by either worldview—that of the hero or that of the saint—becomes a real choice for which we must consciously bear responsibility. It's against this horizon, then, that Camus offers his suggestion that we consider the real possibility of absurdity; against this horizon we can understand more clearly the difference between Sartre and Camus. They differ not over ideas or positions or ideologies, but over methods; how to provoke the crisis of freedom in which alone, they believe, meaning can be discovered. Sartre chooses to emphasize total responsibility as a norm for living authentically, while Camus emphasizes rebellion against the absurdity of the human situation; rebellion, that is, against its subjection to death, its oppression by the totalitarian forces of social conformity that render people incapable of experiencing the fundamental joy or suffering of life.

Camus' own life sheds some light on his singular emphasis on rebellion as an authentic pathway in the human search for meaning, although I would emphasize we should avoid attempting to psychologize away the broader human implications of his work; the ad hominem argument with regard to genius such as Camus' is ultimately a failure of responsibility. Camus was born in Algeria to a French-Algerian settler family. His father died in the battle of the Marne in 1914. Throughout his life, Camus experienced identity conflicts resulting from the colonialism of his environment; he was caught between distinct nationalisms, between differing religious sensibilities, and diverse cultural identities. Gifted intellectually, Camus was dependent on scholarships to pursue his education, and therefore it was constantly clouded by a climate of constant uncertainty: Would he be able to continue or not? A talented soccer player, Camus was stricken with tuberculosis at age 17, ending both his athletic career and threatening to interrupt permanently his studies. The disease afflicted him throughout his life. His personal relationships were troubled and unstable through two marriages and several intense affairs. As a young man, he saw communism as a way of contesting colonial oppression, but later rejected party orthodoxy and moved toward anarchism, joining the resistance during World War II.

In 1942, Camus published his first major works: *The Stranger*, which we'll consider in more detail in a moment, and *The Myth of Sisyphus*, followed by the novel *The Plague* in 1947, and the essay *The Rebel* in 1951. He was awarded the Nobel Prize for literature in 1957. In his first novel, *The Stranger*, Camus asks the reader to imagine living a human life convinced that one's existence was a matter of indifference to the universe, and yet being unwilling to participate in any of the conventions of social expectation that serve to mask this indifferent reality, such as religion, morality, law, and personal commitment. It's important, I think, to see, because again of its—well, the word is appropriate—"strangeness," this novel *The Stranger* is, in a fundamental sense, a challenge and a test of the reader's capacity for imagination; not imagination in the sense of fantasy, conjuring the image of something unreal, but rather imagination precisely as that unique human ability to see more deeply into possibilities for human existence, possibilities for human freedom that are not actual, that do not have the immediacy, the solidity, the security of being in front of us.

The novel opens with its main character Mersault's announcement that "Maman died today. Or yesterday maybe, I don't know." Maman, his mother, he has learned is dead; and yet in a perfectly flat affect his reaction is as if the news made no difference to him or to the world. As the novel progresses, he forms a relationship with a young attractive woman, Marie. They go swimming in the sea on a Sunday afternoon; they become lovers. He likes being with Marie. Later, Mersault, his friend Raymond, and another man, walking on the beach, are followed by two Arabs who seem to be menacing; who are following them because one says that Raymond mistreated his sister. Later, walking alone on the beach, Mersault encounters the two Arabs again. Thinking one of them is threatening him, he takes out a revolver and shoots him once. He's stunned by what he's done, but then, inexplicably, fires four more times. It's important to keep in mind in this brief plot summary that it's the texture of the experience that Camus the novelist creates; his capacity to imagine a virtual reality with a character like Mersault, who in this moment of killing another human being is apparently aware only of the sun beating down on him, the glare of the light in his eyes and the intense heat. They're more real to him than the action of drawing the revolver, shooting, and then deciding to shoot again.

The second part of the book opens with Mersault under arrest for the murder he's committed. During his trial, the prosecutor portrays him as a murderer so heartless that he actually smoked cigarettes at his mother's wake. After his conviction, while awaiting execution, Mersault is visited by a priest who attempts to convince him to repent and to seek forgiveness. Mersault rejects the priest's claim to moral superiority. Let's pay attention to the words with which Camus portrays this moment in the novel. In the voice of Mersault:

> Then, I don't know why, but something inside me snapped. I started yelling at the top of my lungs, and I insulted him and told him not to waste his prayers on me. I grabbed him by the collar of his cassock. I was pouring out on him everything that was in my heart, cries of anger and cries of joy. He seemed so certain about everything, didn't he? And yet none of his certainties was worth one hair of a woman's head. He wasn't even sure he was alive, because he was living like a dead man. ...

> It was as if I had waited all this time for this moment and for the first light of this dawn to be vindicated. Nothing, nothing mattered, and I knew why. So did he. Throughout the whole absurd life I'd lived, a dark wind had been rising toward me from somewhere deep in my future, across years that were still to come, and as it passed, this wind leveled whatever was offered to me at the time, in years no more real than the ones I was living. What did other people's deaths or a mother's love matter to me; what did his God or the lives people choose or the fate they think they elect matter to me when we're all elected by the same fate, me and billions of privileged people like him who also called themselves my brothers? Couldn't he see, couldn't he see that? Everybody was privileged. There were only privileged people. The others would all be condemned one day. And he would be condemned, too. What would it matter if he were accused of murder and then executed because he didn't cry at his mother's funeral?

The power of this moment of revelation in conflict and confrontation with the priest as an obvious symbol of societal expectation, societal morality, convention; the conventions that Mersault claims people use—we all use—to keep death at a distance. But not just physical death, not just the running out of time, but the awareness that we live death constantly because there are no connections to a reality larger than ourselves; we are cut off, as death does, from that reality and from any meaning we might want to think we can find in it, unless we are aware. Once we become aware of being cut off, being absurd, then a possibility opens up; and it's the possibility both of joy and of suffering.

The priest leaves Mersault, and he turns to face his fate, his execution. In it he finds a new sense of life and solidarity; solidarity—ironically, absurdly—with the crowd who greets him with cries of hatred.

> So close to death, Maman must have felt free then and ready to live it all again. Nobody, nobody had the right to cry over her. And I felt ready to live it all again too. As if that blind rage had washed me clean, rid me of hope; for the first time, in that night alive with signs and stars, I opened myself to the gentle indifference of the world. Finding it so much like myself—so like a brother, really—I felt that I had been happy and that I was happy again. For everything to be consummated, for me to feel less alone, I had only to wish that there be a large crowd of spectators the day of my execution and that they greet me with cries of hate.

This extraordinary novel imagines a hero who is alone although he has a mother, a lover, friends, an enemy, a judge, a priest, and a crowd of witnesses to his execution. The hero goes to his death with a kind of certainty, a kind of happiness, and a kind of fellowship with the witnesses to his execution. He is, in other words, the Absurd hero. Mersault's heroism consists of nothing more than this, but of no less than this either: he refuses to lie, or to do what he does not feel or see the reason for. He sees or feels almost nothing but his immediate physical sensation or emotional response to what touches him directly. Mersault enters life, in other words, disarmed; he is in some sense a new Adam, life in its innocence. Why he exists this way we do not know; there is no explanation for the human condition. He lacks the armor of social conventions and ideologies that characterize normal living. In this condition, Mersault is a hero because he does not rely on anyone but himself or on anything that is not his own to avoid facing the possibility that the universe might genuinely be indifferent to his existence and to the existence of whatever is human.

The absurdity of existence that Camus portrays is not a claim about reality, it's not a truth claim, in other words; reality is this way. Rather for Camus, the absurdity is the possibility that our attitudes as human beings toward reality are too simple: faith in meaning, in solidarity, in compassion and love. Even our faith in forgiveness might be simply beside the point, even though it feels as if we could not possibly live without them. Mersault is the hero of the absurd because he does live without them and does not commit suicide, but goes to his death certain of his life and happy with the simple fact of it. That's not possible, we say; there has to be a meaning. Camus asks, "How do you know?"

In a later novel, *The Plague*, Camus portrays a doctor in a quarantined plague-stricken city who lives by a single principle: rebellion against death without illusion of victory. There's a sense in which the doctor, Rieux, in *The Plague* represents a way of life that Mersault could perhaps have followed had he not been executed; a way of life in which he experienced real happiness and fulfillment in engaging in normal human activities without illusion, but in a spirit of conscious rebellion against the reality and the necessity of death.

In one of his later works, *The Myth of Sisyphus*, Camus imagines another, more mythic version of the absurd hero, asking again: Can one actually imagine living happily without meaning? Camus presents Sisyphus, the mythic rebel against death as happy; not through faith, through hope, through love, but through rebellion. The essay begins with the assertion that there is really only one philosophically important question: whether to commit suicide. In other words, Camus seems to ask, can one live life without requiring that living be justified by a meaning or a purpose? Could there be a reason for living in an absurd universe? In fact, think a moment: That's the wrong way to say it. Camus isn't asking if there could be a reason, he's asking can there be a meaning? Can there be a hero's reward for living in a universe that has no reasons; that offers no motive, no purpose, and no goal? Camus makes the point that the heroism of the absurd has its own *arete*—its own heroic virtue—and its own reward in a quality of lucidity and self-certainty. He illustrates this point with the story of Sisyphus who has been condemned forever to push a boulder up a mountain with excruciating effort only to have it to roll back down again and again, forcing him to begin again; an archetype of futility and purposelessness. Quoting from the essay:

> Hence the intelligence, too, tells me in its way that this world is absurd. Its contrary, blind reason, may well claim that all is clear. I was waiting for proof and longing for it to be right. But, despite so many pretentious centuries and over the heads of so many eloquent and persuasive men, I know that it is false. On this plane, at least, there is no happiness if I cannot know. That universal reason, practical or ethical, that determinism, those categories that explain everything are enough to make a decent man laugh. They have nothing to do with the mind. They negate its profound truth which is to be enchained. In this unintelligible and limited universe, man's fate henceforth assumes its meaning. A horde of irrationals has sprung up and surrounds him until his ultimate end. In his recovered and now studied lucidity, the feeling of the absurd becomes clear and definite. I said that the world … itself is not reasonable, that is all that can be said. But what is absurd is the confrontation of the irrational world and the wild longing for clarity whose call echoes in the human heart. The absurd depends as much on man as on the world. For the moment it is all that links them together. It binds them one to the other as only hatred can weld two creatures together. This is all I can discern clearly in this measureless universe where my adventure takes place.

But the story of Sisyphus—his situation of pushing the rock endlessly and futilely uphill—is usually presented without its first act, which Camus supplies. Sisyphus is punished because he scorned death. Dead, he argues his way back to life to avenge a wrong done to him by his wife (shadows and echoes of the Garden of Eden story here); refusing to return as agreed to the underworld, he's condemned to his rock. Camus glosses Sisyphus's story with the claim, "There is no fate that cannot be surmounted by scorn." Let's continue the quotation:

> If this myth is tragic, that is because its hero is conscious. Where would his torture be, indeed, if at every step the hope of succeeding upheld him? The workman of today works

every day in his life at the same tasks, and this fate is no less absurd. But it is tragic only at the rare moments when it becomes conscious. Sisyphus, proletarian of the gods, powerless and rebellious, knows the whole extent of his wretched condition: it is what he thinks of during his descent. The lucidity that was to constitute his torture at the same time crowns his victory. There is no fate that cannot be surmounted by scorn.

If the descent is thus sometimes performed in sorrow, it can also take place in joy. This word is not too much. ... When the images of earth cling too tightly to memory, when the call of happiness becomes too insistent, it happens that melancholy rises in man's heart: this is the rock's victory, this is the rock itself. The boundless grief is too heavy to bear. These are our nights of Gethsemane. But crushing truths perish from being acknowledged. ...

Happiness and the absurd are two sons of the same earth. They are inseparable. ... "I conclude that all is well," says Oedipus, and that remark is sacred. It echoes in the wild and limited universe of man. It teaches that all is not, has not been, exhausted. It drives out of this world a god who had come into it with dissatisfaction and a preference for futile sufferings. It makes of fate a human matter, which must be settled among men.

All Sisyphus' silent joy is contained therein. His fate belongs to him. His rock is his thing. ... One must imagine Sisyphus happy.

Those concluding words: One must imagine the absurd hero condemned to an eternity of futility, of living death, can be happy because of the feel of the rock against cheek and hand, and the experience of certainty and lucidity that the situation gives him. It is his own; he is free with regard to it, and in so being free possesses himself in a way that cannot be taken away by any other reality outside himself. We've pushed the image of the hero as far as we possibly can. In the next lecture, we'll examine the image of the saint, stretched similarly to the breaking point.

Lecture Twenty-Six
Flannery O'Connor and the Mystery of Grace

Scope:

The short stories of Flannery O'Connor offer another perspective on the possibility of finding meaning through a personal relationship even amid what seems to be the utter breakdown and betrayal of the bonds of relationship as a result of inexplicable evil. Marked by an almost uncanny knack for observation and telling detail, O'Connor's stories concentrate our attention on encounters between individual characters in rural southern America, rather than on the level of vast societal violence as in the Holocaust. Through her flair for capturing the grotesque element of life, she probes that mysterious core of human freedom in which both decisive rejection and almost unconscious openness to compassion and forgiveness vie for the hearts and souls of human beings. Beyond understanding, but not beyond the imagination of the artist, O'Connor seeks to offer a last refuge for hope even in the face of the absurd alienation that her recording of daily experiences seem to document in such dense and vivid detail.

Outline

I. Flannery O'Connor's life and literary works are marked by a heightened sense of the tension between dichotomous opposites within individual experience and in society.

  A. O'Connor was born in 1925 in Savannah, Georgia. She died of the hereditary disease lupus in 1964 at age 39.

  B. She wrote 2 novels; 31 short stories, and numerous articles, speeches, and letters.

  C. Her identity as a writer is defined by the peculiarity of her style and subject matter. Sometimes labeled as "Southern American Gothic," her literary voice speaks an idiosyncratic dialect marked by multiple dichotomies.

II. What is most characteristic of O'Connor's literary imagination is its heightened openness to the sense of mystery at the center of human existence, to the Fundamental Human Question, and to the metaphoric structure of the human search for meaning as a question or a commitment.

A. O'Connor's literary imagination reveals her unswerving commitment to mystery as the bedrock of human experience.

B. Her work manifests an acute awareness of the ubiquity of the mysterious and evil at work in human relationships.

C. Her works' emphasis on the grotesque and freakish calls our attention to the roots of violence in the human drive.

D. Perhaps her most intensely focused imaginative genius is revealed in her ability to identify the small but telling details that reveal the profound ambiguity at the center of freedom, equally open to evil and to saving grace.

III. The quality of complementarity, based on the mysterious ambiguity of freedom in its capacity for both evil and grace, repeats in seemingly endless variations throughout O'Connor's stories.

A. In her short story "Revelation," the central character, Mrs. Turpin, experiences a vision that shows her the truth about her racism, moral and social bigotry, and hypocrisy.

B. For O'Connor, like Saint Francis, death is the revelation of the universal poverty that is a fundamental condition of human existence. Death reveals the ultimate insufficiency of individual existence and the absolute need of the other. This universality of need which includes all humanity is the meaning of O'Connor's catholicity.

IV. We find another example of O'Connor's eye for the telling detail in the identical purple hats worn by two women—one white, one black—on a recently desegregated bus in a Southern city.

A. This story, "Everything That Rises Must Converge," is again about dichotomies: mother/son, white/black, and mind/heart.

B. Julian, rationalistic and morally superior in his judgments of his mother, accompanies her to an exercise class. Onboard a city bus, they encounter a formidable black mother and her young son.

C. The black woman knocks Julian's mother senseless with her pocketbook. At first, Julian, who had been humiliated by his mother's prejudice and condescension, is smugly pleased.

D. But as his mother struggles to walk home, refusing to take the bus, Julian is humiliated by his heartlessness and lack of compassion for his mother, whom he now sees is seriously injured, and he runs hopelessly to try to help her.

V. O'Connor portrays the saintly sensibility and the 20th century's struggle to recover a sense of meaning after the confrontation with totalitarianism has made it historically inevitable that the mystery of grace and salvation cannot be partialized so as to exclude any aspect of human existence.

Suggested Reading:

Coles, *Flannery O'Connor's South.*

Fitzgerald, *The Habit of Being.*

O'Connor, *Collected Works* (particularly "Everything That Rises Must Converge" and "Revelation").

————, *Mystery & Manners.*

Questions to Consider:

1. In "Revelation," the person who hurls the book at Mrs. Turpin is a sullen and ugly girl named Mary Grace. Why does O'Connor choose her to deliver the blow to Mrs. Turpin?

2. In "Everything That Rises Must Converge," Julian's mother remarks that she pities people who are half white, saying that they are tragic and must have "mixed feelings." Julian, irritated, protests that he too has mixed feelings. Considering the description of dichotomies in O'Connor's work as discussed in this lecture, how might you interpret this moment?

Lecture Twenty-Six—Transcript
Flannery O'Connor and the Mystery of Grace

In our last two lectures, we've focused on the metaphoric profile of the hero, pushed to its extreme limit by the extensive violence and cumulative force of cultural upheaval in the 20th century. In this lecture and the next, we want to undertake the same profiling for the metaphoric identity of the saint; the saint pushed to its limit and boundary by those same forces and dynamics of cultural change in the 20th century. Our first bit of evidence for this saintly identity at its limit comes from Flannery O'Connor's life and literary works that are marked by a heightened sense of the tension between dichotomous opposites within individual experience and society as a whole. What distinguishes her artistic imagination is an equally heightened awareness of the complementarity between such opposites, giving her work its mysterious character and what I'll refer to in this lecture as its "catholicity." "Catholicity" here comes with a small "c"; it's the universality of her imagination, the ability to take in the whole range of dichotomies and oppositions that characterize human experience. Her catholicity in the narrower sense of the word is also important, but it's the jumping off point for a mysterious reality that lies beyond any confessional distinction or characteristic within saintly identity.

O'Connor was born in 1925 in Savannah, Georgia. She died of the hereditary disease lupus in 1964 at the age of 39. She wrote two novels, 31 short stories, and numerous articles, speeches, and letters. Her identity as a writer is defined by the peculiarity of her style and subject matter. Sometimes labeled as "Southern American Gothic"—"Gothic" in the sense that we associate with a certain type of literature or a certain type of art: gloomy, idiosyncratic, bizarre, somehow menacing or at least disturbing—her literary voice speaks this idiosyncratic dialect that is marked by the multiple dichotomies we've already referred to. Let's detail some of those dichotomies a little bit more specifically. She's a woman writer in a genre marked by very strong male voices concerned with the lost dream of the South; of course most particular among those dominant male voices is the voice of William Faulkner. More generally, she lived in a society that valued traditional gender roles and had very limited tolerance for the peculiar identity of a solitary female who presumed to distinguish her voice from that of others like her. Another element: Her cultural upbringing exposed her to the particular forms of racism that marked the post-Reconstruction, Depression-era rural South.

Furthermore, she was a fervent and intellectually sophisticated Catholic in a dominantly Protestant culture. Diagnosed with lupus at the age of 25 and given about 5 years to live, she struggled with the physical, emotional, and mental constraints of the disease for more than 15 years, during which she produced the largest part of her work. In all of these senses, her identity marked her as "other," differentiating her from those around her.

We can recall here for just a moment the reference with which we concluded an earlier lecture to Simone de Beauvoir, and her identification of otherness as the central characteristic of the identity of woman in the patriarchal history of the West. O'Connor has to be situated not just with regard to her gender but with regard to all of these distinguishing marks of her otherness within the literary history of America in the 20th century. What's most characteristic, I think, of O'Connor's literary imagination is its heightened openness to the sense of mystery at the heart of human existence; openness to what we've referred to in this course as the Fundamental Human Question—Is human existence meaningful or absurd?—as a real question, and an openness to the metaphoric structures of the human search for meaning as a question and as a commitment.

This openness to mystery gives us a moment to pause and reflect just briefly on the way in which we've been operating in a semantic field that is characterized by words like "mystery," "absurdity," "transcendence," and "paradox." All of these words allude to an otherness that is in some way or other beyond the limit of human experience. The particular inflections are important; the difference between a word like "absurdity," for example, for Camus, and "mystery" for O'Connor. And yet it's important to notice that at the same time, they mark a kind of genetic kinship: the preoccupation with what is other? What is completely other; transcendently other? It's a shared characteristic that is heightened by the particular circumstances of culture and society that we're observing.

As we've said, O'Connor's literary imagination reveals her unswerving commitment to mystery as the bedrock of human experience. Her stories trace the protean ways in which, as she said, mystery proves to be "a great embarrassment to modern man." Her work manifests an acute awareness of the ubiquity of the mysterious and of the murderous evil at work in human relationships, as well as the mysterious power of love and relationship. Across the canvas of her familiar rural southern countryscape, she depicts scenes of horror and also of beauty that on a microcosmic scale are analogous on the one hand to the killing fields of Flanders and Verdun, Dunkirk, Dresden, and Hiroshima; and on the other hand, to scenes of beauty in human experience that cannot be repressed by what is dark and foreboding. The emphasis in her works on the grotesque and the freakish forcefully calls our attention to the roots of violence in the human drive to heighten differences so as to reinforce self-identity in reference to the other through mechanisms of demonization. We hear echoes in this of Camus in *The Stranger*; that necessity society feels to urge convention, to urge familiarity, normalcy on the experience of the individual.

Some examples of this resistance to normalcy, this eruption of the bizarre in the work of O'Connor: We can note, for example, in a character like that of the hermaphrodite in one of her best-known short stories, "A Temple of the Holy Ghost"; this freak of nature who needs to be kept at a distance, kept in a carnival, because somehow the ambiguity of gender identity, the ambiguity of opposite traits of the masculine and the feminine within each and every one of us is too frightening, too disturbing, too unsettling, too uncertain to be dealt with as part of everyday experience. Another example: The serial killer in "A Good Man Is Hard to Find" who identifies himself only as "the Misfit," emphasizing that the serial killer, if you will, in all of us must be outside the bounds of ordinary civil society, mustn't it? Another example: the "cloud of witnesses" ascending into Heaven in the story "Revelation"—which we'll look at more closely in a moment—represents a triumphant host which includes, she says, "white trash, black niggers in white robes, and battalions of freaks and lunatics." O'Connor put it this way herself: "The freak in modern fiction is disturbing to us because he keeps us from forgetting that we share in his state."

Perhaps her most intensely focused imaginative genius is revealed in her ability to identify that small but telling detail—the garish color of an outlandish hat—reveals the profound ambiguity at the center of freedom; we'll follow that example through later on in the lecture in the context of one particular story. But that revealing detail that shows itself to be open equally to evil and to saving grace; thus she embodies the reconciliation in her own imagination of the Protestant sensibility that surrounded her, and the Catholic sensibility in which her own spirituality was fostered. This dichotomous emphasis between works on the one hand (the Catholic sensibility) and faith alone (the Protestant sensibility) and the ambiguity between the two that we've discussed to some extent in previous lectures are things to be taken at face value; or can their meaning only be perceived through faith and the way in which that dichotomy ripples out through the way in which people organize not only their religious lives but their social values as well? She put it this way; again quoting her: "Freedom … is a mystery … [that] cannot be conceived simply … and one which a novel … can only be asked to deepen. … Free will does not mean one will, but many conflicting wills in one man."

This is that quality of complementarity that we've seen before both in quantum physics and also in the phenomenology of Sartre; that complementarity that is based on the mysterious ambiguity of freedom in its capacity for both evil and grace; both meaning and absurdity. It repeats itself in seemingly endless and delightful variations throughout O'Connor's stories. In her short story, "Revelation," the central character, Mrs. Turpin, experiences a vision that shows her the truth about her racism, moral and social bigotry, and hypocrisy. In the story, the vision is preceded by a wonderful scene in a doctor's waiting room where Mrs. Turpin is forced into proximity with people she considers riff-raff. She observes that "there's a heap of things worse than a nigger," shouting, "Thank you Jesus" every time she realizes how much more fortunate she is than these others, and that she's not so ugly, so ill-bred, and freakish as they are. Her exclamations goad one of her fellow patients to fling a book that strikes her full in the head, rendering her senseless.

In wonderful unspoken irony, this turns out to be the "good book" because it will have the effect of knocking some sense into Mrs. Turpin's head. The grace delivered by the blunt force trauma of the "good book" is revealed only after she's returned home. As she tends to her pigs—this is her profession—she is furious at God for her humiliation in front of a jeering crowd of "white trash and niggers." She gazes for a long time into the pigpen and then her vision is transformed. In Mrs. Turpin's vision, the calvary of the waiting room, where she thinks of herself as crucified the way Jesus was, is transformed first into the purgatory of her daily labor, her time among the pigs, and then into the host of witnesses who are ascending into heaven, with her and her kind bringing up the rear. Let's listen now to his wonderful scene in the inflections of O'Connor's own voice:

Then like a monumental statue coming to life, she bent her head slowly and gazed, as if through the very heart of mystery, down into the pig parlor at the hogs. They had settled all in one corner around the old sow who was grunting softly. A red glow suffused them. They appeared to pant with a secret life.

Until the sun slipped finally behind the tree line, Mrs. Turpin remained there with her gaze bent to them as if she were absorbing some abysmal life-giving knowledge. At last she lifted her head. There was only a purple streak in the sky, cutting through a field of crimson and leading, like an extension of the highway, into the descending dusk. She raised her hands from the side of the pen in a gesture hieratic and profound. A visionary light settled in her eyes. She saw the streak as a vast swinging bridge extending upward from the earth through a field of living fire. Upon it a vast horde of souls were rumbling toward heaven. There were whole companies of white-trash, clean for the first time in their lives, and bands of black niggers in white robes, and battalions of freaks and lunatics shouting and clapping and leaping like frogs. And bringing up the end of the procession was a tribe of people whom she recognized at once as those who, like herself and Claude, had always had a little of everything and the God-given wit to use it right. She leaned forward to observe them closer. They were marching behind the others with great dignity, accountable as they had always been for good order and common sense and respectable behavior. They alone were on key. Yet she could see by their shocked and altered faces that even their virtues were being burned away. She lowered her hands and gripped the rail of the hog pen, her eyes small but fixed unblinkingly on what lay ahead. In a moment the vision faded but she remained where she was, immobile.

At length she got down and turned off the faucet and made her slow way on the darkening path to the house. In the woods around her the invisible cricket choruses had struck up, but what she heard were the voices of the souls climbing upward into the starry field and shouting hallelujah.

Mrs. Turpin's vision wonderfully expresses what I've termed O'Connor's catholicity, which has little if anything to do directly with doctrine or denomination, but everything to do with an inclusiveness based on the universal poverty of the human condition. For O'Connor, like Saint Francis, death is the revelation of the universal poverty that is the fundamental condition of human existence. Death reveals the ultimate insufficiency of individual existence and the absolute need of the other. We hear in her echoes of the voice of Father Zossima from *The Brothers Karamazov*. This universality of need that includes all humanity is the meaning of O'Connor's catholicity.

We find another example of O'Connor's eye for the telling detail in the identical purple hats worn by two women—one white, one black—on a recently desegregated bus in a Southern city. In this story, "Everything That Rises Must Converge," we find once again those dichotomies, those tensions between opposites that are so characteristic of her fiction. For example: the tension between mother and son, between white and black, between mind and heart. Julian, a rationalistic and morally superior young man, is judgmental with regard to his mother. He accompanies her to her exercise class. Onboard a city bus, they encounter a formidable black mother and her young son. The black woman is wearing the same ornate hat as Julian's mother. Julian's mother is torn between humiliated racial pride that this black woman can sit near her and wear the same hat as she on the one hand; and an instinctive and quite genuine warm-heartedness toward the little boy, to whom she wishes to give a nickel, but can only find a penny. Stung by what she takes to be this condescension on the part of Julian's mother, the black woman knocks her mother senseless with her pocketbook. At first, Julian, who had been humiliated by his mother's prejudice and condescension, is smugly pleased. But as his mother struggles to walk home, refusing to take the bus, Julian is humiliated by his heartlessness and lack of compassion for his mother, whom he now sees is seriously injured, perhaps dying, at the onset of a stroke—it's unclear in the story—and he runs hopelessly to try to help her. Let's pick up the story at this point. In Julian's voice we hear:

> "Don't think that was just an uppity Negro woman," he said. "That was the whole colored race which will no longer take your condescending pennies. That was your black double. She can wear the same hat as you, and to be sure," he added gratuitously (because he thought it was funny), "it looked better on her than it did on you. What this all means," he said, "is that the old world is gone. The old manners are

obsolete and your graciousness is not worth a damn." He thought bitterly of the house that had been lost for him. "You aren't who you think you are," he said. …

"You needn't act as if the world had come to an end," he said, "because it hasn't. From now on you've got to live in a new world and face a few realities for a change. Buck up," he said, "it won't kill you."

She was breathing fast.

"Let's wait on the bus," he said.

"Home," she said thickly.

"I hate to see you behave like this," he said. "Just like a child. I should be able to expect more of you." He decided to stop where he was and make her stop and wait for a bus. "I'm not going any farther," he said, stopping. "We're going on the bus."

She continued to go on as if she had not heard him. He took a few steps and caught her arm and stopped her. He looked into her face and caught his breath. He was looking into a face he had never seen before. "Tell Grandpa to come get me," she said.

He stared, stricken.

"Tell Caroline to come get me," she said.

Stunned, he let her go and she lurched forward again, walking as if one leg were shorter than the other. A tide of darkness seemed to be sweeping her from him. "Mother!" he cried. "Darling, sweetheart, wait!" Crumpling, she fell to the pavement. He dashed forward and fell at her side, crying "Mamma! Mamma!" He turned her over. Her face was fiercely distorted. One eye, large and staring, moved slightly to the left as if it had become unmoored. The other remained fixed on him, raked his face again, found nothing and closed.

"Wait here, wait here!" he cried and jumped up and began to run for help toward a cluster of lights he saw in the distance ahead of him. "Help, help!" he shouted, but his voice was thin, scarcely a thread of sound. The lights drifted farther away the faster he ran and his feet moved numbly as if they carried him nowhere. The tide of darkness seemed to sweep him back to her, postponing from moment to moment his entry into the world of guilt and sorrow.

O'Connor portrays the saintly sensibility and the 20th century's struggle to recover a sense of meaning after the confrontation with totalitarianism has made it historically inevitable that the mystery of grace and salvation cannot be partialized so as to exclude any aspect of human existence. None can be saved unless all are saved, O'Connor seems to testify, and to refuse salvation for all is to refuse salvation for oneself as well. In this, O'Connor echoes, as I noted before, the spirit of forgiveness we saw embodied in Saint Francis of Assisi, and at the same time joins her voice to that of both de Beauvoir and Camus in the call for total responsibility. Her way of putting it, in one of her addresses, "One can only see into the depths of one's self when he or she experiences limitation or poverty, the bedrock of all human experience."

O'Connor's saint is a peculiar, even bizarre, grotesque figure in its multiple incarnations throughout her stories; but the one thing all of her saintly characters share is the need to recognize that they are not alone, not just in the sense that they are supported by a power beyond themselves, by the bonds of community, but they're not alone in their need to give their lives a meaning, their need to find something that they can identify as their own. They share this with every other human being, and that fundamental need—the need that expresses itself as the question: What does life mean; what is it all about; is it about anything?—that question and the commitment that life demands of us to pursue it is the poverty that she speaks of, that poverty that is itself the mystery of our existence, the poverty that comes upon all because all, in the end, come up short, run out, realize they are not other, they are not unique, they are not privileged; the realization that, as Dostoevsky put it, all are responsible to all, for all; all owe a death to every other, a death not in the form of a sacrifice but a death that surrenders itself, acquiesces to pass on into the others, as a kind of food. This is that Eucharistic image that we proposed as the alternative to a sacrificial understanding of the religious bond; the fact that we can and must feed one another, not just from our abundance but from our poverty. O'Connor forces us to recognize through the freakishness of her characters that it is the human condition itself that is freakish—Camus would cause it absurd—that life must share itself through death with all other life.

Lecture Twenty-Seven
The Holocaust and the Crisis of Forgiveness

Scope:

This lecture returns to the metaphor of the saint through an examination of 20th-century writers who address the search for meaning amidst the trauma of unimaginable evil from within the Jewish tradition of religious and ethical concern. First, we consider Buber's radicalization of the promise/covenant basis for human identity in the relationship of person to person as he explored it in his famous book, *I and Thou*. Next we turn to Emmanuel Levinas whose work *Totality and Infinity* can be seen as an attempt to turn philosophy from its rootedness in the impersonal worldview of Greek culture to a radical personalism in which the face-to-face encounter of human beings is the origin of identity and the structure of a meaningful life. Finally, a discussion of Elie Wiesel's novel *Night* brings to a focus the question: Is it possible to restore the bond of human relationship once it has been decisively broken by evil? Or, "Did forgiveness die in the death camps?"

Outline

I. In this lecture we continue our reflection on the dynamics of totalitarianism in the 20th century by considering the Holocaust and its implications for the human search for meaning.

    A. Of the approximately 72 million deaths in World War II, nearly 11 million civilians were killed in Nazi death camps.

    B. Like the atomic bomb, the Holocaust raises the realistic possibility of a human choice to annihilate humanity.

    C. The question of a radical mutation in the cultural evolution of the meaning of responsibility raises a further question about forgiveness, which we have identified as being at the heart of the saint's identity.

II. The life and career of Martin Buber, Jewish theologian and philosopher, offer a useful perspective on what might be called the crisis of modern Judaism.

    A. In addition to scholarly writings, Buber pursued a revival of religious consciousness among Jews through imaginative retellings of Hasidic tales, an evocative German translation of the Bible, and active leadership of the Zionist movement.

B. Buber promoted a social-utopian agenda for Zionism, including the establishment of a bi-national Arab and Jewish state as a resolution of the conflict in Palestine.

C. Buber distinguishes between two fundamental and dichotomous modes of human relationship: the "I-Thou" and the "I-It."

III. Emmanuel Levinas, Russian-born philosopher who lived primarily in France, carries forward a program to reshape the very identity of philosophy by converting it from the province of the hero into the homeland of the saint.

A. Levinas's philosophical project is often characterized by the phrase "ethics as first philosophy."

B. To some significant extent, this can be understood in terms of Buber's "I-Thou/I-It" dichotomy.

C. His main legacy for philosophy is a shift of priorities away from knowledge toward ethical responsibility to the other.

D. Levinas distinguished himself from Buber by emphasizing a responsibility to the other that precedes dialogue and communication, a responsibility that is absolute in virtue of the absolute otherness to which the self is responsible for the very possibility of its own identity.

IV. Elie Wiesel's account of his journey through the death camps simultaneously recapitulates and calls into question the scriptural story of God's covenant with the children of the promise.

A. *Night* opens with an exchange between the 16-year-old Eliezer and Moishe the Beadle, a comic figure who sees more than others. He instructs the boy on secrets of the Kabbalah, the arcane mystical writings of Judaism.

B. Soon, everything in Elie's life is brought into question, most urgently his relationship to God.

C. His whole family is shipped in cattle cars to Auschwitz. Immediately, there is a selection of those who will die, including his mother and sister. The experience changes Wiesel forever.

D. Throughout months of internment, Elie manages miraculously not to be separated from his father. As his father grows increasingly helpless, the boy's attitude toward him weakens with his father's failing will to live. Finally, days before the liberation of the camp, Elie watches helplessly as his father succumbs.

E. In Wiesel's story, we see the climactic inversion of the story of faith from its beginning with Abraham to its conclusion in Elie's reversal of the sacrifice of Isaac, Job's calling of God to account, and finally including even the hyperbolic repetition of the demand for sacrifice in the death of Jesus.

F. Witness to God's silence in the face of the burnt offering of 6 million sacrificial victims, Elie breaks the bond of the covenant and puts an end to the patience of Job.

G. Rejecting dialogue with God as "Thou," he searches for a more humanly proportioned responsibility than that demanded by Levinas.

V. In one sense we can view the trajectory from Buber, through Levinas and Wiesel, as pointing toward not only the uncertain and unresolved question of the present and future identity of Judaism but of scriptural monotheism.

A. Scriptural religion is called into question by totalitarianism's power to imagine and enact the death of humanity.

B. The question of total forgiveness hangs over the history of scriptural religion and its persuasive rootedness in Western culture. But what would such forgiveness look like?

C. Wiesel offers only a veiled and tentative hint in his Nobel Prize speech. He appeals to memory as the source of hope: hope for the future in the memory of the past.

Suggested Readings:

Marcel, *The Philosophy of Existentialism.*

Rilke, *Letters to a Young Poet.*

Tillich, *The Courage to Be.*

Questions to Consider:

1. There has been much debate about whether *Night* should properly be classified as a memoir or a novel. Why do you think Wiesel told his story in the way that he did?

2. Wiesel refers to Job in his Nobel speech as "our ancestor, our contemporary." How does Job's ordeal differ from Wiesel's?

Lecture Twenty-Seven—Transcript
The Holocaust and the Crisis of Forgiveness

In this lecture, we continue our reflection on the dynamics of totalitarianism in the 20th century by considering the Holocaust and its implications for the human search for meaning. It's in the context of the Holocaust that we're able to discern the metaphoric profile of the saint at its extreme limit. Of the approximately 72 million deaths in World War II, nearly 11 million civilians were killed in Nazi death camps; 6 million were victims of the Third Reich's "Final Solution of the Jewish Question." Like the use of the atomic bomb in Japan, the Holocaust raises the realistic possibility of a human choice to annihilate humanity itself. With World War II, the notion of "crimes against humanity" becomes a question that for the first time humans must take responsibility for, and must recognize as a genuine question for which their freedom must take account. The question of a radical mutation in the cultural evolution of the meaning of responsibility raises a further question within the context of saintly identity about forgiveness, which we have already identified as being at the heart of that identity; the central question for the saint's self-identification through love. Is forgiveness, in the end, the final and complete meaning of love?

Our reflection in this lecture, then, is to be based on the testimony of the Jewish religious and cultural tradition in response to the Holocaust. First, we consider Martin Buber's contribution to the emergence of a radically personalist conception of human existence. Next, we explore how Emmanuel Levinas draws on this personalist emphasis and moves it in the direction of a reshaping of philosophy, replacing the Greek metaphysical emphasis on theoretical science and knowledge with an ethical concern for responsibility to others. Finally, we conclude by reflecting on the personal testimony to the Holocaust by Elie Wiesel. In particular, we look to Wiesel for help in formulating the question of the possibility of total forgiveness parallel to the concept of total responsibility we saw emerge with French existentialism; total forgiveness for the destruction of humanity by humanity, and whether such forgiveness could ever be regarded as being responsible. The question of a possible responsibility for total forgiveness will require us to consider how this responsibility might extend to include God as well as human beings.

So we begin first with Martin Buber: The life and career of Martin Buber, Jewish theologian and philosopher, offer a useful perspective on what might be called the crisis of modern Judaism. In addition to scholarly writings, Buber pursued a revival of religious consciousness among Jews through imaginative retellings of Hasidic tales, an evocative German translation of the Bible, and active leadership of the Zionist movement. Buber, a powerful orator who enjoyed great popularity as a visionary and prophet, promoted a social-utopian agenda for Zionism, including the establishment of a bi-national Arab and Jewish state as a resolution of the conflict in Palestine.

Early in his career, Buber published his best-known work, *I and Thou*. In it, Buber distinguishes between two fundamental and dichotomous modes of human relationship: the "I-Thou" and the "I-It." The "I-Thou" relationship implies an openness to the reality of the other as such; an openness that Buber insisted went beyond language's ability to encompass. On the other hand, this is not to say that Buber thought that such an ineffable relationship was either mystical or abstract; it was a concrete, living encounter at the level of personal existence marked by genuine, mutual recognition. The "I-Thou" encounter could take place between persons in a variety of different modalities, but it could also occur between humans and nature, and also with God; the "I-Thou" relationship, in other words, speaks to a quality of presence as its fundamental characteristic. Buber highlights the "I-Thou" relationship as allowing a depth of experience of meaning that is impossible within the "I-It" relationship. From Buber we take this concern for a need to reawaken in humanity, and particularly within the context of the Jewish tradition, this capacity for presence that Buber saw as recreating the faith discovery of Abraham in his experience of Covenant relationship.

Emmanuel Levinas, Russian-born philosopher who lived primarily in France, carried forward a program to reshape the very identity of philosophy by converting it from the province of the hero into the homeland of the saint. Levinas's philosophical project, in other words, can be characterized very effectively by the phrase "ethics as first philosophy." Let's dwell upon the significance of that characterization. To some significant extent, this notion of "ethics as first philosophy" can be understood in terms of Buber's "I-Thou/I-It" dichotomy. Levinas's main legacy for philosophy is a shift of priorities away from knowledge toward ethical responsibility for the other. This is a conversion of philosophy from the love of wisdom to the wisdom of love, as Levinas sees it. Levinas distinguished himself from Buber by emphasizing a responsibility to the other that precedes dialogue and communication; it doesn't depend upon a person-to-person encounter, although that is, of course, the form in which Buber wanted to suggest it's most genuinely realized. Levinas wanted to emphasize a prior responsibility that is absolute in virtue of the absolute otherness to which the self is responsible for its own very possibility of identity; we owe ourselves to the other, he would say.

The relationship that Levinas describes as "the face-to-face encounter with the other" constitutes the very nature of subjectivity, in other words; of every Self to every other. We see how close this comes to that other great portrayal of saintly identity we saw in Father Zossima by Dostoevsky: all are responsible to all for all. But there's something more, for Levinas, at stake here: an extension of that universal responsibility to a quality of absoluteness as well; a responsibility that has the absolute quality of Abraham's encounter with the God who promised the gift of life through the covenant relationship of exclusive fidelity, that relationship of absolute uniqueness: the one true God, the one chosen people. Levinas's insistence on the absolute character of the responsibility to the other raises again the paradoxical question, which we found originally in the Abraham story, of the demand for sacrifice, the demand for a gift of death that seems inseparable from the story of the origins of the covenant relationship.

With the scene thus set, Elie Wiesel's account of his journey through the death camp simultaneously recapitulates and calls into question the scriptural story of God's covenant with the children of the promise. Wiesel's memoir *Night* opens with an exchange between the 16-year-old Eliezer—his given name—and Moishe the Beadle, a comic figure, at least initially, who sees more than others do. He instructs the boy on secrets of the Kabala, the arcane mystical writings of Judaism. Soon, however, everything in Elie's life is brought into question, most urgently his relationship to God. His whole family is shipped in cattle cars to Auschwitz. Immediately, there is a selection of those who will die, which, it turns out, will include his mother and sister. The experience changes Wiesel forever. Let's listen to the account, in his own words, of that night:

Never shall I forget that night, the first night in camp, that turned my life into one long night seven times sealed.

Never shall I forget that smoke.

Never shall I forget the small faces of the children whose bodies I saw transformed into smoke under a silent sky.

Never shall I forget those flames that consumed my faith for ever.

Never shall I forget the nocturnal silence that deprived me for all eternity of the desire to live.

Never shall I forget those moments that murdered my God and my soul and turned my dreams to ashes.

Never shall I forget those things, even were I condemned to live as long as God Himself.

Never.

Later in the story, he witnesses with all of the camp inmates the execution of a young child by hanging. The child, it turns out, is not heavy enough for the fall to break his neck so he lingers in agony, and the prisoners are forced to file past the weeping, staring eyes of the hanged child. Wiesel recounts the scene this way; referring to the hanging figure he says:

And so he remained for more than half an hour, lingering between life and death, writhing before our eyes. And we were forced to look at him at close range. He was still alive when I passed him. His tongue was still red, his eyes not yet extinguished.

Behind me, I heard the same man asking:

"For God's sake, where is God?"

And from within me, I heard a voice answer:

"Where He is? This is where—hanging here from this gallows. ..."

That night, the soup tasted of corpses.

Throughout the long months of internment, Elie had managed miraculously not to be separated from his father. As his father grows increasingly helpless, however, the boy's attitude toward him weakens with his father's failing will to live. Finally, days before the liberation of the camp, Elie watches helplessly as his father succumbs. He says:

> I heard his voice, grasped the meaning of his words and the tragic dimension of the moment, yet I did not move.
>
> It had been his last wish to have me next to him in his agony, at the moment when his soul was tearing itself from his lacerated body—yet I did not let him have his wish.
>
> I was afraid.
>
> Afraid of the blows.
>
> That was why I remained deaf to his cries.
>
> Instead of sacrificing my miserable life and rushing to his side, taking his hand, reassuring him, showing him that he was not abandoned, that I was near him, that I felt his sorrow, instead of all that, I remained flat on my back, asking God to make my father stop calling my name, to make him stop crying. So afraid was I to incur the wrath of the SS.
>
> In fact, my father was no longer conscious.
>
> Yet his plaintive, harrowing voice went on piercing the silence and calling me, nobody but me.
>
> "Well?" The SS had flown into a rage and was striking my father on the head: "Be quiet, old man! Be quiet!"
>
> My father no longer felt the club's blows; I did. And yet I did not react. I let the SS beat my father, I left him alone in the clutches of death. Worse: I was angry with him for having been noisy, for having cried, for provoking the wrath of the SS.
>
> "Eliezer! Eliezer! Come, don't leave me alone. ..."
>
> His voice had reached me from so far away, from so close. But I had not moved.
>
> I shall never forgive myself.

> Nor shall I ever forgive the world for having pushed me against the wall, for having turned me into a stranger, for having awakened in me the basest, most primitive instincts.

> His last word had been my name. A summons. And I had not responded.

In Wiesel's story, we see the climactic inversion of the story of faith from its beginning with Abraham to its conclusion in Wiesel's reversal of the sacrifice of Isaac: now the son sacrifices the father. The reversal of Job's calling of God to account: Wiesel says he will never call God to account for this, there can be no forgiveness. Finally, it even extends to include the hyperbolic repetition of the demand for sacrifice in the death of Jesus. Witness to God's silence in the face of the burnt offering of six million sacrificial victims, Elie breaks the bonds of the Covenant and puts to an end the patience of Job. Rejecting "I-thou" dialogue with God, he searches for a more humanly proportioned responsibility than the kind of total responsibility demanded by Levinas.

As the story moves to its conclusion, Wiesel says:

> But now, I no longer pleaded for anything. I was no longer able to lament. On the contrary, I felt very strong. I was the accuser, God the accused. My eyes had opened and I was alone, terribly alone in a world without God, without man. Without love or mercy. I was nothing but ashes now, but I felt myself to be stronger than this Almighty to whom my life had been bound for so long. In the midst of these men assembled for prayer, I felt like an observer, a stranger.

In one sense, we can view the trajectory from Buber through Levinas and Wiesel as pointing toward not only the uncertain and unresolved question of the present and future identity of Judaism, but the uncertain future of scriptural monotheism as a whole. One of the things we've been concerned to emphasize in our study is that it is not Judaism or Christianity or Islam that is the particular focus of our concern and investigation, but the very idea of scriptural religion as such; to use an abstract word, the monotheism that arises from the singularity of the Covenant formed by Abraham. It is that entire homogeneous experience—the experience of the saint, the saint who defines him or herself wholly with the love and by the love of the other—that is called into question here. Scriptural religion is called into question by totalitarianism's power to imagine and enact the death of humanity as such. Once again, we need to remind ourselves that this notion of a "crime against humanity"—the notion of the death of humanity as such—is not a matter of quantity, nor is it the matter of empirical fact; it's a matter of the imagination's capacity to take in a horizon of meaning that threatens to dwarf it completely, to render it absolutely speechless and absolutely silence, to render day night in which nothing can be seen.

But at the same time we recognize in this possibility of the death of humanity the reality of the experience of mystery itself. This is the truth; the truth of reality that is unspeakable, impenetrable, beyond words, beyond gestures, beyond faith, and beyond practice.

The specter of total death necessarily includes the death of God at the hand of humanity as the redeeming price for God's demand of sacrificial death for sin; but whose sin? Who is guilty of crimes against humanity? Wiesel says it is God as much as the Nazis. So the question becomes: Can either be forgiven; or did forgiveness die in the death camps? The power of this question of total forgiveness hangs over the history of scriptural religion at its moment of crisis in the mid-20th century and continues with us today; continues with us in its persuasive rootedness in the entirety of Western culture. But what would total forgiveness look like? How could it be imagined? Wiesel offers only a veiled and tentative hint in this direction in his words from his Nobel Prize acceptance speech in 1986. There, he says:

> Job, our ancestor. Job, our contemporary. His ordeal concerns all humanity. … He demonstrated that faith is essential to rebellion, and that hope is possible beyond despair. The source of his hope was memory, as it must be ours. Because I remember, I despair. Because I remember, I have the duty to reject despair. …

> There may be times when we are powerless to prevent injustice, but there must never be a time when we fail to protest. …

> Mankind needs to remember more than ever. Mankind needs peace more than ever, for our entire planet, threatened by nuclear war, is in danger of total destruction. A destruction only man can provoke, only man can prevent. Mankind must

remember that peace is not God's gift to his creatures, it is our gift to each other.

Wiesel appeals to memory as the source of hope; hope for the future that within Christianity is identified with the idea of Resurrection that, we have seen, arises as the gift of forgiveness. For Wiesel, that hope for the future arises in the memory of the past; but which memory? For Wiesel, of course, the answer is clear: the memory that is seared into his consciousness; seared into his very being. The memory that encapsulates all memories, all history, the entire history of the Covenant and turns it into a matter not to be settled as with Job between God and man, but as Wiesel says here, between man and man. A human matter; not so much to the exclusion of God, but as a kind of withdrawing of the privilege that the status of God confers; of being somehow or other different, being somehow or other "other," apart from and beyond the reach of the implications of sin, of the demand for sacrifice, of the need for forgiveness. Total forgiveness is the forgiveness of all for all. For Wiesel, at least as we try to interpret, the direction in which his words and the Nobel Prize address are headed, perhaps gropingly, perhaps tentatively and uncertainly, the messianic promise for him seems to lie precisely in the memory of the death of innocents and the death of God that their sacrifice brought about.

Has Wiesel forgiven himself? Could he consider forgiving the Nazis? Could he forgive God? Could he forgive all who failed him as he failed them in the moment of the death of his father? At least as I read it, the Nobel lecture leaves the question entirely open; and for that act of courage—the courage to leave the question open—it seems to me Wiesel deserves not simply our human admiration, respect, and profound compassion but a deep debt of gratitude for witnessing to the necessity, to allow the question of freedom: saintly freedom, yes; freedom in the form of forgiveness; forgiveness as the ultimate expression of love, a willingness to hold open the possibility whether it to be to God, other human beings, or even to ourselves. And yet at the same time, having lived and always remembering to always continue to live the other possibility as well: The possibility that forgiveness did in fact die in the death camps.

Lecture Twenty-Eight
Faulkner and Beckett—Images of the Forlorn

Scope:

Two of the most original and challenging writers of the 20th century are William Faulkner and Samuel Beckett. Faulkner's *The Sound and the Fury* and Beckett's *Waiting for Godot* offer revealing attempts to reimagine Shakespeare's great tragedy, *King Lear*, which considers the human person in the extreme condition of "forlornness." Stripped of all the external trappings of social status and cut off from the bonds of loyalty and affection, Lear on the heath prefigures and prophesies the situation of the Compton family for Faulkner and of Estragon and Vladimir for Beckett. Taken together these three images reveal the vector that, from the perspective of the 20th century, we can now see was present from the very beginning of the modern period in Western culture: a growing awareness that human existence cannot mask its naked exposure to death and that it is the forlornness and bereavement of death that finally poses the true question of the meaning of life.

Outline

I. In this lecture we focus on Samuel Beckett's best-known work, his play *Waiting for Godot*, and on William Faulkner's great novel, *The Sound and the Fury*. By proposing a stylistic and thematic connection to Shakespeare's *King Lear*, we attempt to clarify another central element of heroic identity in the 20th century: human existence as "forlorn."

II. King Lear on the heath offers a powerful metaphor for the human condition in which the search for meaning must be lived out.

    A. Lear first invokes the fury of nature to augment his bitter anger over the ingratitude of his daughters. Then in response to the Fool's solicitude for him, Lear recognizes that he is not alone in wretchedness and bears some responsibility not just for his own situation, but as king, for that of others whom he has neglected.

B. Lear has gone mad on the heath; after Cordelia is executed in prison, the play ends with Lear, returned to sanity, carrying her dead body and lamenting over her until he too dies of grief.

C. The father's lament over the child who has been sacrificed so that he might be redeemed recalls the central pattern that we have identified in the worldview of the saint.

III. We revisit Lear's heath in Samuel Beckett's *Waiting for Godot*.

A. Beckett is able to bring into play a range of mythologies and social conventions, through his minimalist style and disregard for the conventions of linear plot and character development.

B. The play involves two characters—Vladimir and Estragon—who are simply "waiting for Godot," an otherwise unidentified and unseen character. The only action occurring is their encounters, one in each of the play's two acts.

C. Because of the extreme minimalism of Beckett's dramatic style, the players' characters and their situation invite interpretation through the conventions and associations of an almost unlimited number of meaning structures: religious, moral, social, sexual, and existential.

D. Ironically, however, it is the very richness of interpretive possibilities that defeats interpretation.

IV. In *The Sound and the Fury*, Faulkner struggled with the art and craft of writing to open up new paths of access in consciousness to this experience of the human search for meaning that lies beneath both the cultural mythologies and conventional roles that substitute themselves as answers for the lived experience of the questions which human existence itself is.

A. The structure of Faulkner's novel makes it apparent stylistically that none of the Compsons' individual stories can be separated from the stories of the others or from their past and future.

B. This interweaving is not for the purpose of creating a clearer, more complex, or more intelligible master-narrative, but rather to demonstrate no single, coherent meaning can be discovered that would be true to the texture of the novel.

C. In the fabric of Faulkner's story, present time takes on the texture and feel of lived experience, a flow of time without decisive climax or enlightenment.

V. In the 20th century, the art of figures like Faulkner and Beckett endeavors exhibit the virtue of endurance.

Suggested Reading:

Beckett, *Endgame*.

———, *Waiting for Godot*.

Faulkner, Nobel Prize acceptance speech.

———, *The Sound and the Fury*.

Karl, *William Faulkner*.

Questions to Consider:

1. Recalling our earlier discussions of Greek tragedy, consider how the medium of drama, whether Shakespearean or minimalist, shapes the portrayal of the theme of the forlorn in the plays discussed here.

2. Does the concept of existence as "forlorn" translate into the saintly worldview? How?

Lecture Twenty-Eight—Transcript
Faulkner and Beckett—Images of the Forlorn

In our last several lectures, we've been outlining the profile of hero and saint at the limit to which those archetypes—those pathways on the human search for meaning—have been pressed in the 20th century by the sheer force of what we've termed totalitarianism; not simply a political or a social movement, but those fundamental realities in their interaction that shape our existence as a whole, that shape it ultimately mysteriously. In this lecture, we want to focus on Samuel Beckett's best-known work, his play *Waiting for Godot*, and on William Faulkner's great novel, *The Sound and the Fury*. By proposing a stylistic and thematic connection between these two works and Shakespeare's *King Lear*, we hope to attempt to clarify another central element of the situation of saint and hero at the limit in the 20th century; I'm going to use the term to identify that dynamic, that element, that situation of being at the limit: designate it as the condition of being "forlorn." We'll first attempt to clarify the sense in which we might understand the human condition in its occurrence, its situation in the 20th century, as "forlorn" by examining Shakespeare's portrayal of King Lear, specifically that situation in which Lear finds himself in the center of the play on the heath. Then we'll trace some close parallels to this scene that can be found in Beckett's *Waiting for Godot*, arising from what critics have referred to as his stylistic "minimalism." Then we'll move on to consider how Faulkner's treatment of time and narrative in *The Sound and the Fury* reveals a somewhat less apparent but equally telling characteristic of the human condition as "forlorn."

The significance of emphasizing the artistic portrayal of the human condition as "forlorn"—the reason we're focusing on these works in this particular way—is to bring our attention squarely to the implications of one particular aspect of the cultural environment, the cultural milieu, the cultural habitat that the 20th century inhabits, and the way in which that habitat affects the process of cultural evolution for both hero and saint during this same period of time. The world of the hero, as we have seen, is one of solitary exposure to the mysterious forces that shape the universe; this solitary exposure is the basis of the idea of forlornness that we're going to examine: exposure to forces that are at one and the same time overpowering and yet indifferent. This exposure, then, leads to the extreme vulnerability of the human condition with which it's ill-equipped to cope; being exposed is something that this animal, the human, is not well-equipped to deal with. Unless protected by heroic virtue, the forces of nature and society to which humanity is exposed leave it in that condition of extreme destitution and debilitation that we're here terming "forlorn."

King Lear on the heath offers a powerful metaphor for the human condition in which the search for meaning must be lived out. In Act III, Scenes 2 and 4 of the play, Lear first invokes the fury of nature to augment his own bitter anger over the ingratitude of his daughters. He says at one point: "Blow, winds, and crack your cheeks! rage! blow! / You cataracts and hurricanoes, spout."

Then, in response to the Fool's solicitude, this expression of concern for him, Lear has a realization, a moment of clarity; he recognizes that he is not alone in wretchedness, and he bears some responsibility not just for his own situation, but as king, for that of others whom he has neglected. Lear says:

> Poor naked wretches, wheresoe'er you are,
> That bide the pelting of this pitiless storm,
> How shall your houseless heads and unfed sides,
> Your loop'd and window'd raggedness, defend you
> From seasons such as these? O! I have ta'en
> Too little care of this! Take physic, pomp;
> Expose thyself to feel what wretches feel,
> That thou mayst shake the superflux to them,
> And show the heavens more just.

Lear recognizes that it is his responsibility, not just as king but simply as a human being; the Fool is able to awaken that dimension of his humanity for him, to expose himself to feel what wretches feel because all are wretched. Shortly after this, Lear has gone mad on the heath; and as the play evolves moving towards its conclusion, he discovers that Cordelia has been executed in prison. The play ends with Lear, returned to a semblance of sanity, carrying her dead body and lamenting over her until he, too, dies of grief. The image of Lear bearing the dead body of Cordelia and placing it down on the stage has to evoke in us the image of Michelangelo's *Pietàs* that we discussed in an earlier lecture; it's the same scene with a gender inversion. At that point, Lear says:

And my poor fool is hang'd! No, no, no life!
Why should a dog, a horse, a rat, have life,
And thou no breath at all? Thou'lt come no more,
Never, never, never, never, never!
Pray you, undo this button: thank you, sir.
Do you see this? Look on her, look, her lips,
Look there, look there!

Look there; but what does he see? Her lips moving; breath; or the absence? Like Michelangelo's last *Pietà*, this *Pietà*, this Shakespearean parent and child in the moment of death remains utterly ambiguous. The father's lament over the child who has been sacrificed so that he might be redeemed recalls the central pattern that we've identified in the worldview of the saint; so we're not just considering the heroic worldview but recognizing the necessary intermingling of the two. Together in its forlorn condition, this image of humanity exposed to naked poverty—that naked poverty that ultimately Saint Francis referred to as "Sister Death"—this exposure of humanity and its heartbreaking vulnerability to necessity we're left to contemplate with the question: What does it mean? Does it mean?

With that image as our backdrop, we turn now to Beckett's *Waiting for Godot*, first performed in 1953; and in doing so, I think it's important to recognize that we are revisiting Lear's heath. The curtain opens on the play, a barren landscape with a tree at the center of it, and we're tempted to say, "We're back in the Garden of Eden. Here's Adam and Eve in the person of Vladimir and Estragon, and this is the situation." Tempting; but Beckett doesn't allow anything to be that straightforward. Through his minimalist style and his disregard for the conventions of linear plot and character development, Beckett is able to bring into play a wide range of mythologies and social conventions, all of which we're quite tempted to say, "Ah, there it is; this is the Genesis story. This is the story of Cain and Abel." Not just biblical stories: heroic stories, and yet at the same time stories of oppression; stories of social faulthood; stories of social pretense, the unmaking of pretense and the need to find something beyond it. But none of these stories are sufficient in the reality of the drama to shield the characters from the apparent absurdity of their basic forlorn condition.

Beckett, born in Ireland in 1906, wrote both in English and French, reflecting his identification with both countries. He was closely associated with James Joyce, whom he admired and respected, but also from whom he wanted to distance himself. He fought in the French Resistance during World War II, and won the Nobel Prize for Literature in 1969. He's often considered the central figure in the "Theater of the Absurd" movement in 20th century drama. As we know, the play involves two characters, Vladimir and Estragon, who are simply "waiting for Godot," an otherwise unidentified and unseen character. The reason for the appointment, which goes unkept throughout the play, is not given. The only action that occurs are their encounters, one in each of the play's two acts, with Pozzo and Lucky, two other characters whose relationship is apparently either master and servant or, in Pozzo's characterization, master and slave.

In the midst of that basic plot outline, a series of exchanges among the four characters begins to establish a repetitive but fascinatingly varied pattern. It often goes something like this:

> But that's not the question. Why are we here, that is the question. And we are blessed in this, that we happen to know the answer. Yes, in this immense confusion, one thing alone is clear. We are waiting for Godot to come.

> We wait. We are bored. No, don't protest, we're bored to death, there's no denying it. Good. A diversion comes along and what do we do? We let it go to waste. … In an instant all will vanish and we'll be alone once more, in the midst of nothingness!

The Irish theater critic Vivian Mercer famously said of the play that it achieves the impossible: a riveting play that keeps audiences on the edge of their seats in which nothing happens, twice! She's observing that the first act and the second act mirror one another with only the most subtle kinds of variations, and in both cases it's nothing that happens. That happening of nothing has to recall for us Sartre's phenomenological analysis of consciousness that we discussed in basic terms in a previous lecture. Sartre basically sees freedom in the way in which nothing happens; it's not simply an absence of event, it's a space, an open space, this nothing; this forlorn condition of being on the heath in which meaning can happen, but first there must be a question: not only what does it mean; does it mean? Because of the extreme minimalism of Beckett's dramatic style, the players' characters and their situation invite interpretation through the conventions and associations of almost an unlimited number of meaning structures: religious (the Genesis story in the background), moral, social, sexual, and existential. As I'm sure we well know, interpretations have abounded; but ironically, it's the very richness of interpretive possibility that with regard to this play—and with regard to the larger experience of human existence and culture that it typifies—that in the end defeats interpretation. There are too many possibilities; too many interpretive stories that can be plausibly associated with these characters and what little they reveal of themselves. The play in a sense plays at seduction, teasing the human sensibility to search for meaning in a situation that constantly resists and refuses to give any; in that sense, it portrays the human condition of being exposed to mystery, and in that condition being forlorn.

We turn now to Faulkner, and the extraordinarily important place he plays not only in 20th century American literature but in the dynamics of culture in that century altogether. In his 1949 Nobel Prize acceptance speech, Faulkner said that young writers of that time suffered the tragedy of being so burdened by the fear of being blown up—the atomic bomb—that they had forgotten (his words) "the problems of the human heart in conflict with itself," which he said was the only subject matter worth writing about. In *The Sound and the Fury*, written 20 years before the Nobel Prize speech, Faulkner had struggled with the art and craft of writing to open up new paths of access in consciousness to this experience that we've been discussing of the human search for meaning that lies beneath both the cultural mythologies and conventional roles that substitute themselves for the lived experience of the question itself—the questions that are posed when human existence finds itself in question; in conflict with itself without clarity about either its situation or its direction.

Of course as is well known, the title of the novel is taken from Shakespeare's *Macbeth*, specifically from that moment in Act V, Scene 5, when Macbeth realizes that everything that he thought was true of his choices and his accomplishments has turned into (his words) "a tale told by an idiot, full of sound and fury, signifying nothing"; which is, of course, the same nothing that Vladimir and Estragon were busy doing in their own play. Despite his plans and accomplishments, of course, Macbeth finds himself at the end of the play forlorn like Lear on the heath, a condition both characters share—although in very different identities—with the members of the Compson family who are at the center of Faulkner's novel. The structure of Faulkner's novel makes it apparent stylistically that none of the Compson's individual stories can be separated from the stories of any of the others or from their past and their future. In a certain sense, the primary protagonist of Faulkner's novel is time itself, and the relationship of time to narrative; narrative as the way time happens.

But it doesn't happen linearly for Faulkner; his interweaving of character, voice, and event without regard for the conventions of chronological development or logical progression is not for the purpose of creating a clearer, more complex, or more intelligible master-narrative, but rather to demonstrate that no single, coherent meaning can be discovered that would be true to the texture of the novel as a whole. Not only are these siblings—the Compson family: three brothers and a sister, and structurally at least (I think the similarity extends further) but just in time of bare structure we can't help recognizing the similarity of configuration with Dostoevsky's *Brothers Karamazov*. I think, as I suggested, the similarity goes much deeper; not perhaps on a conscious level of imitation but in terms of the resonance that's created—lost in one another, but also in the myths with which their lives are saturated: the myths of Christianity (the novel opens on Good Friday and moves toward Easter); the myth of lost southern gentility and chivalry; and the distinctly Southern version of the American myth of progress, prosperity, and pride, a myth that, in Faulkner's perception, is ironically but unmistakably sustained by the endurance and the will to survive of black former slaves. In that recognition, we sense the presence of another great American novel of a somewhat earlier time: Mark Twain's *Huck Finn*. There is that same concern with the Southern-American experience of the human condition that we saw as a central concern of Flannery O'Connor in an earlier lecture.

The novel is structured in four parts, each with a different narrator. The first three parts are conveyed in the voices of the Compson brothers: First, 33-year-old Benjy, who is emotionally and behaviorally profoundly disabled, and who presents his experience of Good Friday, 1928. Second, the oldest brother, Quentin, on what proves to be the day of his suicide by drowning while he's a student at Harvard, an event that took place 18 years earlier than Benjy's episode. Third, there's Jason, the youngest brother; avaricious, devious to the point of dishonesty, resentful, and humanly impotent, though in a different sense than Benjy, who had been castrated as a result of a misadventure with some schoolgirls when he was younger. Finally, the fourth part of the novel is narrated by an anonymous voice that knows more than any of the characters individually, but doesn't rise to the level of omniscience; the narrator does not know enough to be able to synthesize their stories, to put them in sequence either chronological or in the sequence of case and effect that would establish a stable meaning. It's only able to accomplish a limited synthesis by piecing them together around a central character: Dilsey, the matriarchal black servant who does as much as can be done to keep the family functioning; something only she can do.

The boys' sister, Caddy, has no voice of her own in the novel; and of course this is powerfully significant. Her story exists only by being woven through that of her brothers in various tonal keys. We sense here, again, resonance with Simone de Beauvoir's analysis of the identity of woman as the other to the male in *The Second Sex*. To Benjy, Caddy is mother; to Quentin, she is lover; to Jason, she is whore. But as Faulkner's imagination makes clear, she is none of these things; none of the roles she plays in men's stories capture her identity. Like Dilsey, her own role is to endure and to hold together what is broken without being able to heal it.

In the fabric of Faulkner's story, present time slips indiscernibly into the past and back again until the weave of characters and events takes on the density of lived human experience, which is not chronological; which is not linear in its narrative structure. In Faulkner's art, the portrayal of these characters and their experiences and their polyphonic voices—again, there's a strong similarity between Faulkner's narrative style and that of Dostoevsky in this polyphonic quality that critics of both writers have commented on frequently— multiplicity of voices, but also a multiplicity of tonalities within those voices, all interweaving in a kind of symphony, but a symphony like all music that arises out of nowhere, returns to nowhere, and holds itself together in its meaning we could say (although we're not talking about verbal meaning; conceptual meaning) but in its identity holds itself together solely in the momentary interrelationship of the notes, the characters in this case, the events. This polyphonic quality to Faulkner's work, like Dostoevsky's, is the only sense in which—the novel seems to suggest—human experience is able successfully to resist being conventionalized or mythologized in a linear narrative with a beginning, middle, and an end; a protagonist and villain; as a comedy or a tragedy. The purpose of the writing is to resist that reduction of human experience to an explanation, a reason, a pattern of cause and effect; and in this, once again, we encounter, we touch back to the experience of Camus' *Sisyphus*, or to *The Stranger*, for whom events are not a patterned framework on which meaning is to be constructed but rather a series of happenings, the point of which is that they only happen.

For Faulkner, the pattern of events and the voices of the character take on the texture and feel of lived experience; a flow of time without decisive climax and without enlightenment. It is only lived, and as such is forlorn, searching for meaning that never appears except in the infinitely varied yet clearly recognizable patterns that are familiar to all of us as the way in which our history, the history of our culture, has tried to express, has tried to probe and question, as Faulkner said, the "problems of the heart in conflict with itself." In the 20th century, in the midst of the upheaval of totalitarian forces that threaten to undo the tenuous bonds of meaning that identify personal and social relationships, the art of figures like Faulkner and Beckett endeavors—like Sisyphus straining against his rock—to exhibit the virtue of endurance as that bedrock, and perhaps also the peak, that the human search for meaning must situate itself upon.

As human existence is further and further exposed to the stormy forces of dissolution that have gathered in these troubled times of the 20th century, heroic excellence becomes flattened out, stripped down naked to a refusal to yield. In the art of the forlorn, of those who endure the struggle and whose victory seems only to be that they will not be defeated, this art presents what it takes to be the fundamental human condition, as well as the fundamental human question. Their meaning—to the degree that it has a meaning; in the sense that their meaning is in question—is their endurance; and because their meaning endures, it becomes a kind of eternal truth, the same kind of eternal truth that Camus suggests Sisyphus experiences when Camus says, "We must imagine Sisyphus happy." Because in that quality of endurance, in the feel of the rock against the face, the hand that braces the rock, there is certainty; a certainty of an existence that endures, both suffers and maintains itself in that suffering, and knows its truth.

Lecture Twenty-Nine
Viktor Frankl—Freedom's Search for Meaning

Scope:

In a brief but gripping memoir entitled *Man's Search for Meaning* Viktor Frankl, an Austrian psychiatrist and Holocaust survivor, replicates Socrates' *Apology* by translating Socrates' notion of the "care of the soul" into a more contemporary language and situating it in an encounter with a contemporary monstrosity of evil. This lecture offers a reading of Frankl's journey through the death camps and considers the prize which he brought back to the community in the form of "logotherapy." Logotherapy, Frankl's version of the care of the soul, confronts the reader, with the necessity to make a decision about the role that freedom, responsibility, and suffering play in the human search for meaning in life.

Outline

I. Viktor Frankl's *Man's Search for Meaning* can be understood as a translation of Socrates' principle of the "care of the soul" into the more contemporary idiom of the human search for meaning.

II. We consider Frankl's discussion of the human search for meaning in terms of three basic elements: freedom, responsibility, and suffering.

    A. Frankl articulates the sense in which he identifies freedom as the source of meaning in one of the most frequently quoted statements in the book.

    B. This unalienable freedom I take to be the same reality that Socrates refers to as the "soul."

    C. According to Frankl, the equivalent to Socrates' body/soul distinction is the distinction of freedom from liberty of choice.

        1. Liberty of choice refers to the way that we deal with external, circumstantial situations.

        2. Freedom is the capacity of each person to decide what his or her identity as a person will be, by deciding the principles by which his or her way of living will be guided and how they will be applied in specific circumstances of choice.

D. Frankl's point is that in the camps the prisoners' liberty of choice was stripped away; they were forlorn. Their freedom, however, remained their own.

III. Human freedom functions as responsibility.

A. Frankl articulates this sense of the basic human condition or situation as one of "being in question;" that is, being responsible, in terms reminiscent of Socrates, making clear that life does not so much have a meaning but is in search of meaning.

B. The structure of responsibility for life's questions clarifies further what "meaning" itself means. When we describe human existence as a search for meaning, we do not refer to ideas, beliefs, or even truths in any propositional sense. "Meaning" is relationship.

C. Frankl draws out the implication of what it means to be responsible by emphasizing that the meaning of life will vary from person to person and will develop dynamically through the course of a lifetime.

D. In this notion of responsibility we recognize the specifically heroic character of Frankl's approach to the question of the meaning of life.

IV. Frankl distinguishes his style of psychotherapy, which he called logotherapy, from Freudian psychoanalysis by identifying a basic source of meaning that Freud neglects: suffering.

A. The word "suffering" must be understood etymologically here to comprehend the full meaning of Frankl's assertion.

1. A passion is the opposite of an action. One initiates an action; one undergoes or suffers a passion.

2. All sensations and emotions are passions; they are the reactions of the senses and feelings to the impressions things and people make on us.

3. From this perspective, it is clear that we must regard love, or joy, for example, as sufferings. I do not decide to love someone or rejoice over something. The person or the event makes me, by its beauty or goodness, love or rejoice.

B. Understood thus, it becomes clear that by far the greatest part of human existence occurs as suffering rather than action.

C. If one cannot find meaning in what one suffers, then by far the greatest part of life is doomed to meaninglessness.

D. Suffering is given meaning by the way in which it is accepted, passionately.

E. Death is the final passion of every human life. Death becomes meaningful when it is passionately accepted.

V. Frankl's conception of the human search for meaning through freedom, responsibility, and the passionate acceptance of suffering grew out of and in response to the forlorn extremity of human existence in face of totalitarian terror.

A. Frankl's stance toward the search for meaning is radically heroic in that it is rooted in the person's responsibility to oneself for oneself.

B. At the same time, Frankl's approach is profoundly saintly even though it can function fully independently of any conception of a personal relationship between human existence and divine mystery.

C. Passionate acceptance of suffering regardless of its nature or origin gestures toward the idea of suffering as gift and toward freedom as necessity.

D. Frankl's conception of the human search for meaning therefore prefigures the identity of the secular saint.

Suggested Reading:

Frankl, *Man's Search for Meaning*.

Frankl, *The Will to Meaning*.

Viktor Frankl Institute for Logotherapy website:

http://www.logotherapyinstitute.org/

Questions to Consider:

1. Compare Frankl's outlook on the search for meaning to doctrines of various religions. For example, how does his concept of freedom versus liberty of choice fit in with the historic debate over free will and predestination?

2. How do Frankl's ideas compare to the views of other saintly figures, both those discussed in this course and others?

Lecture Twenty-Nine—Transcript
Viktor Frankl—Freedom's Search for Meaning

Viktor Frankl's book *Man's Search for Meaning* can be understood as a translation, a kind of updating to the language and mindset of the 20th century, of Socrates' principle of the "care of the soul," allowing it to speak in a new time and a new cultural situation with the same power that Socrates did to the Athenians in his own time. Both Frankl and Socrates view human existence as a process of being questioned by life and having to decide what meaning we shall attribute to it through the way in which we live. By exploring this connection between Socrates and Frankl, we'll take one final step toward sketching out another aspect, another perspective on the profile, of the secular saint; the metaphoric figure who will guide us in bringing the course of our study of the contribution of philosophy and religion to the human search for meaning in our own time and our own place to the conclusion that we will reach, less a conclusion really than a place we must stop so as to begin again.

Viktor Frankl, Viennese psychiatrist and Holocaust survivor, wrote a memoir—*Man's Search for Meaning*—that has been ranked among the 10 most influential books of the 20th century in America. An estimated 20 million copies in more than 25 languages have been sold worldwide. In my experience teaching introductory philosophy courses at Georgetown, I have seldom encountered a student who did not find the book remarkable; for many, it' proven life-changing. The book's power and its credibility seem to stem from its simple and direct testimony to what Frankl identifies as the most basic and enduring form of human freedom: the freedom every person always has, despite everything, to find and affirm meaning in one's own life, on one's own way. Frankl's testimony was born of the interplay in his own life between a fate he shared with millions and a personal response uniquely his own.

Prior to his internment with his wife and parents in the concentration camp in 1942, Frankl had established a brilliant reputation for success in identifying those at risk for suicide and in developing effective therapeutic techniques. In 1946, shortly after his liberation from a death camp near Dachau, Frankl published the first version of the memoir that eventually became *Man's Search for Meaning*. The book was first published in English in 1959. In this lecture, we'll consider Frankl's discussion of the human search for meaning in terms of three basic elements: freedom, responsibility, and suffering.

Frankl articulates the sense in which he identifies freedom as the source of meaning in one of the most frequently quoted passages in the book. Frankl says:

> We who lived in concentration camps can remember the men who walked through the huts comforting others, giving away their last piece of bread. They may have been few in number, but they offer sufficient proof that everything can be taken from a man but one thing: the last of the human freedoms— to choose one's attitude in any given set of circumstances, to choose one's own way.

This unalienable freedom I take to be the same reality that Socrates refers to as the "soul"; the object that Socrates exhorted his fellow citizens to take care of above all else. As such, it must be identified in the same way that Socrates did the soul in its most basic terms: For Socrates, the soul is, number one, different than the body; number two, more important than the body. According to Frankl, the equivalent to this body/soul distinction that Socrates makes is the distinction between freedom and liberty of choice. This will help bring into focus something we touched on in our earlier lectures where we discussed Socrates: body and soul in that context of Plato's thought have to be thought of not as two separate things, one material the other spiritual, but rather as two value systems—metaphors if you will—of two different ways of living, specifically two different ways of making choices. For Frankl, liberty of choice refers to the way in which we deal with external, circumstantial situations. It's a little bit like a restaurant menu: Every situation that we find ourselves in constitutes a set of options among which we may choose, while at the same time excluding all other options. There are some things in a given situation that are possible; the same situation makes many other things impossible. We get to choose from among the available options. Liberty of choice, in other words, is our capacity to select for ourselves without arbitrary constraint from among the options that are or at least should be available to us in a particular situation.

Many times when we're discussing this matter in class I'll startle some students and get some raised eyebrows in return when I say this is, of course, what's meant by our Declaration of Independence, declaring that among the things they take to be self-evident is that human beings all have an inalienable right to life, liberty, and the pursuit of happiness; because liberty is for the sake of the pursuit of happiness. Therefore it becomes clear that the only thing that any government of any social institution can confer on its citizens is liberty; governments, social institutions have nothing to do ever, under any circumstance with freedom. The business of social organization is to establish, safeguard, and promote liberty of choice, which is different than freedom. Freedom has to do with the capacity that each person has to decide what his or her identity as a person will be; an identity that is not external, that is not tangible, and that is not situational but is a matter of meaning. Freedom allows us to decide the principles by which we will make our way through life, by which our way of living will be guided; and how those principles will be applied in specific circumstances of choice. Freedom, in other words, as Frankl is using the word, is freedom of conscience; the ability to choose one's own way. No one, no thing, no society, no institution confers or takes away freedom of consciences; it is our unique and sole possession. Frankl's point is that in the camps the prisoners' liberty of choice was entirely stripped away; they were forlorn. Their freedom, however, remained their own.

Our second thematic issue in this consideration of Frankl's book: Freedom functions as responsibility. You recall that we first encountered Frankl back at the very beginning of the course of our lectures, and Frankl served a function at that point of focusing our attention with regard to the search for meaning in the profile of both the saint and the hero, in terms of the idea that the search for meaning is a matter of a question and a commitment to live that question. It's from that notion of questioning as the fundamental human commitment that this notion of responsibility first arose and has been the organizing leitmotif, the unspoken central concern at the heart of much we've been talking about. The circumstances and events of life, together with the choices and the actions of other human beings, constitute in Frankl's view the situation in which a person exists. Our situation can be understood as articulating a question directed to us as free; that question: What response will I choose to make to my situation; what does my situation mean? What meaning will I attribute to it through the relationship I decide to have with it; a relationship that is not a matter of ideas, but rather a relationship that is established through concrete, specific attitudes, choices, actions, and commitments?

Frankl articulates this sense of the basic human condition or situation as one of being in question—that is, being responsible—in terms reminiscent of Socrates, making clear that life does not so much have a meaning but is a search for meaning. Frankl puts it this way, speaking about the situation in the concentration camp:

> What was really needed was a fundamental change in our attitude toward life. We had to learn ourselves and, furthermore, we had to teach the despairing men, that *it did not really matter what we expected from life, but rather what life expected from us.* We needed to stop asking about the meaning of life, and instead to think of ourselves as those who were being questioned by life—daily and hourly. Our answer must consist, not in talk and meditation, but in right action and in right conduct. Life ultimately means taking the responsibility to find the right answer to its problems and to fulfill the tasks which it constantly sets for each individual.

The structure of responsibility for life's questions, rooted in freedom, clarifies further what "meaning" itself means. When we describe human existence as a search for meaning, we're not, as I said a moment ago, referring to ideas, beliefs, or even truths in any propositional sense. "Meaning" is relationship; "meaning" is the way situations, things, and persons interact with, relate to, and configure themselves in relation to one another. We are responsible for the way we relate to our situation and to other persons. These relationships are the living meaning of life.

Frankl draws out the implication of what it means to be responsible by emphasizing that the meaning of life will vary from person to person, from situation to situation, and will develop, change, ebb, and flow dynamically through the course of a lifetime. The meaning of human life is both absolutely unique and at the same time purely individual; it's shared with all other persons, and yet at the same time it's uniquely our own. In this we can sense the common source of the image of both hero and saint. The hero is alone; each of us is alone with our responsibility for our freedom and the identity we choose. We share that condition of being alone with our freedom with every other human being; and this, it seems to me, is the particular genius of Frankl's reflection on the meaning of his own experiences in the camps. He expresses that concern—that question—as he experienced it in words like these:

> These tasks, and therefore the meaning of life, differ from man to man, and from moment to moment. Thus it is impossible to define the meaning of life in a general way. Questions about the meaning of life can never be answered

by sweeping statements. "Life" does not mean something vague, but something very real and concrete, just as life's tasks are also very real and concrete. They form man's destiny, which is different and unique for each individual.

Yet, as we have seen, that unique fate that must be decided by each individual is the condition that all human beings share. This will become, as we'll see in a moment, the basis for the very profound meditation that Frankl carries on not only in this work but in all of his voluminous writings on the importance of human suffering and compassion.

In this notion of responsibility, then, we recognize the specifically heroic character, as we've said, of Frankl's approach to the question of the meaning of life. Within the context of his own Jewish faith, he recognizes that the meaning of one's life is a matter of one's own responsibility for oneself to oneself. Let me pause for a moment and just clarify the significance of that relationship between Frankl's both ethnic and religious identity as a Jew, and his profession as a man of science, a psychoanalyst and a psychotherapist. We see in this the suggestion that we'd begun to raise about the coexistence, the tension between the hero and the saint, within one person's identity and within one person's experience. Psychoanalysis and psychotherapy insofar as is it a science functions within the heroic worldview, the Greek worldview. Frankl's own formation within the traditions and culture of Judaism functions within the worldview of the saint. Frankl has no problem moving back and forth between these two; I would suggest because he instinctively sees them for the metaphoric realities that they are and their constantly therefore in dialogue for him. Let's explore that a little further.

Frankl distinguishes his style of psychotherapy, which he called logotherapy—that is, "meaning-therapy"—from Freudian psychoanalysis by identifying a basic source of meaning that Freud that he felt Freud neglected: human suffering. Quoting Frankl:

> Thus far we have shown that the meaning of life always changes, but that it never ceases to be. According to logotherapy, we can discover [this] meaning in life in three different ways: (1) by creating a work or doing a deed; (2) by experiencing something or encountering someone; and (3) by the attitude we take toward unavoidable suffering.

I believe that Frankl's emphasis on the freedom of one's response to unavoidable suffering accounts for his book's stunningly wide appeal, as well as constituting the basis for his pivotal role in the direction that our own course here will now be taking. Let me emphasize for a moment that it is crucial that we focus on the precise words Frankl uses for the role that he attributes to suffering in the process of the human search for meaning; he emphasizes that it is when we encounter "unavoidable suffering." Frankl would be the first to recognize, I think, that there are unfortunately, perversely a myriad of ways in which we create as human beings suffering for ourselves. That's not what he's talking about; what he's talking about are those forms of suffering that happen to us, and we'll probe that notion a little bit further.

As a survivor of the same horrors to which Wiesel was exposed, and as a psychiatrist who specialized in suicide prevention, Frankl is uniquely capable of diagnosing the forlorn condition of humanity that we reflected on in the last lecture; diagnosing it as forlorn in the face of totalitarian terror, terror at the realistic possibility of the death of humanity, the reality of the crimes against humanity that our century has witnessed over and over again, raising the possibility of the death of the human search for meaning itself, the death of meaning, the death of forgiveness, the death of the very possibility of being human. Frankl says at a certain point:

> When a man finds that it is his destiny to suffer, he will have to accept his suffering as his task; his single and unique task. He will have to acknowledge the fact that even in suffering he is unique and alone in the universe. No one can relieve him of his suffering or suffer in his place. His unique opportunity lies in the way in which he bears his burden.

It seems to me piercingly clear that in saying that, Frankl is saying exactly the same thing that Camus was saying to us about the relationship of Sisyphus to his rock: His rock, Camus says, is his thing; his moira; his fate; assigned uniquely and inescapably to him. But the meaning of his relationship to the rock, what the feel of the rock against his cheek and hand means, that, too, is his. The image of Sisyphus, in other words, is an image of the human condition as forlorn, but forlorn in a condition of suffering. The word "suffering" as we're using it here—as Frankl uses it and as we're attempting to elaborate its meaning—has to be understood etymologically, I think, in order to comprehend the full significance of what Frankl is saying. The Latin root of the word that's translated into English as "suffering" is equivalent to the root from which we get the word in English "passion"; the Latin is the word *patior*, it's past participle, *passus*, means "to suffer." "Passion," in other words—the way in which suffering happens—is the opposite of an action: action/passion. With regard to action, an action is an event that I initiate; when I act, I take the initiative. With passion, on the other hand, it is an event that happens to us; we undergo it or suffer it. What I do is an action; what happens to me through external agency is a passion. All sensations and emotions are passions; they are caused by something other than ourselves and they happen to us. They are the reactions of the senses and the human feelings to the impressions things and people make on us. Some of these reactions are pleasurable, some painful; all are passions. We suffer pleasure just as we suffer pain.

Once again, this is one of those points where in class with the students with the introduction to philosophy eyebrows are raised, puzzled glances are exchanged; what is he talking about? Pleasurable suffering as opposed to painful suffering; what does that mean? A basic human reality, the mystery of which Frankl wants to probe with regard to its capacity to create meaning; Frankl's basic point is suffering, in a fundamental sense, has to be seen as a gift— paradoxical as that assertion may be—because it gives us opportunities for meaning where otherwise they would not exist. From this perspective, it's clear that we must regard love, or joy, for example, as sufferings in the sense that Frankl is using the word. I do not decide to love someone; I do not decide to rejoice over something; the person or the event makes me by its beauty or its goodness, love or rejoice. Love and rejoicing are sufferings.

Understood in this way, it becomes clear that by far the greatest part of human existence occurs as suffering rather than action. Birth and death, most of what comes between those two events, happens to us; we suffer our life, we suffer our death in the most fundamental sense. If one cannot find meaning in what one suffers, then—Frankl makes the point—by far the greatest part of life is doomed to meaninglessness. Suffering is given meaning by the way in which it is accepted; for Frankl, passionately. Death is the final passion of every human life. Death becomes meaningful when it is passionately endured.

Frankl's conception of the human search for meaning through freedom, responsibility, and the passionate acceptance of unavoidable suffering grew out of and in response to the forlorn extremity of human existence that he experienced in the death camps. Frankl's stance toward the search for meaning is, in a fundamental sense as we have learned to see, radically heroic in that it's rooted in the person's own responsibility for him or herself to him or herself; the responsibility each of has for our own identity rooted in the absolute freedom of conscience. At the same time, Frankl's approach is also profoundly saintly even though it can function fully independently of any conception of a personal relationship between human existence and a divine mystery; it doesn't presume a conception of God, in other words, although it is completely open to it. saintliness in this sense, for Frankl, has this basic characteristic we've identified from the very begin: the idea of conceiving human existence primarily in terms of personal relation. Frankl's saintliness arises out of the role that he attributes as central to suffering, to the passion of life, and specifically to compassion; compassion as an expression of love, a certain kind of relationship, a certain way of sharing the human search for meaning that is built into the very structure of human existence itself.

Passionate acceptance of suffering regardless of its nature or origin—regardless of how we understand the context in which it occurs: theistically, atheistically, or in some other way; scientifically—gestures toward the idea of suffering as gift and toward freedom as necessity. Every gift is the gift of freedom; meaning originates in freedom. Freedom is absolute necessity; without freedom there is no meaning. Freedom is both personal as gift-giving, the mutuality of gift-receiving, and equally impersonal; the necessity that must always be as it is prior to and apart from any specific meaning. Frankl's conception of the human search for meaning, therefore, prefigures the identity of the secular saint; the direction in which our investigation has gradually been evolving for itself as we've proceeded through this discussion of the 20th century: The secular saint as a type of human existence that passionately accepts the necessary suffering of living as both hero and saint, but without the ambition to convert one into the other and in conscious recognition of the impossibility of any reconciliation between the two identities. In our remaining lectures we'll try to flesh out this profile of the secular saint and examine the way in which it does or does not aid us in our search for meaning in our time and our place.

Lecture Thirty
Simone Weil—Imagining the Secular Saint

Scope:

Though less well known than her French contemporaries Sartre and de Beauvoir, Simone Weil gradually emerged in the second half of the 20th century as representing a genuinely radical and original stance toward the question of life's meaning: a refusal to choose between the hero and the saint. Weil's life reveals a frightening yet inspiring attempt to live the truth of both paths to meaning fully and simultaneously, with full awareness of the terrifying human risk involved. This lecture begins with a biographical sketch of Weil's life, which reveals a complex identity full of contradictions, and then goes on to examine the principal influences on her intellectual formation and early writing. Among the factors examined are her passionate attachment to Greek culture and philosophical thought, especially Plato, and an equally passionate, almost driven commitment to radical reform and social justice.

Outline

I. With the introduction of the secular saint we break new ground, both in this course and, to some extent, in cultural discourse.

   A. We may characterize secular saint as an ideal type of person who lives the question of meaning in human existence fully open to its mystery and fully committed to searching for meaning along the paths of both the hero and the saint.

   B. We must acknowledge that, as we have presented these two paths and their historical development, they are mutually exclusive opposites that resist synthesis or assimilation

   C. This makes the figure of the secular saint an embodiment and affirmation of the human person primarily in terms of his or her freedom of conscience exercised as an absolute responsibility for one's identity in relation to the mystery of reality as a whole.

II. Simone Weil has been widely regarded as a creative genius by figures as diverse as Albert Camus, T. S. Eliot, Paul Tillich, Hannah Arendt, Dorothy Day, Robert Coles, and Charles de Gaulle.

    A. Weil was born in Paris in 1909; she died at age 34 in a sanatorium in Kent, England, of tuberculosis, complicated by her refusal of food to demonstrate solidarity with those in Nazi-occupied France.

    B. She suffered from a weak constitution and severe physical ailments throughout her life, especially chronic debilitating headaches. She was both physically and socially awkward and ruthlessly self-critical.

    C. Her brief life was bracketed by the two world wars and shaped by the political, social, and economic dislocations that dominated the years between them. She registered the anguish of her times with exquisite sensitivity and felt obligated to rethink Europe's collapsing civilization.

    D. In the last five years of her life a mystical spiritual perspective unexpectedly opened to her. She came to know the love of God as intimately, she said, as the smile of a friend.

III. Simone Weil's thoughts on the political and economic dynamics of society have their roots in Greek philosophy and reflect the characteristics of the heroic worldview and the concept of heroic citizenship that evolved from it.

    A. Weil's conception of justice is simple and straightforward: Justice, she says, consists in seeing that no avoidable harm is done to any person.

    B. Weil understands human existence as a whole, and questions of justice specifically, in the context of the impersonal worldview of Greek philosophy.

    C. She articulates this vision most clearly in one of her last works, the essay "Draft from a Statement of Human Obligations." Weil designates the essay a "profession of faith."

    D. The essay's worldview, like Plato's, is divided into the separate realms of body and of soul.

E. The only possible link between the two realms of body and soul is human freedom, the capacity every person always has to consent or withhold consent to direct attention beyond the world to that transcendent good, which alone can wholly satisfy the fullest desire of the heart.

IV. Weil's conception of justice is based on the strict obligation of every person to do all in his or her power to meet the needs of both body and soul of every other person.

  A. The notion of obligation is pivotal for Weil's idea of justice because it is the expression of absolute respect for that desire for transcendent good in the soul of every person.

  B. Respect for the universal desire for total good cannot be shown directly; it is not tangible. On the other hand, unless the respect is enacted it is meaningless.

  C. The needs of the body are food, shelter, clothing, and physical security. The needs of the soul are meaning and value, rooted in freedom of conscience.

  D. Weil distinguishes sharply between human needs and preferential desires.

  E. Weil uses the term "affliction" to designate an intensity of suffering, whether naturally or deliberately caused, that does harm not only to personal sensibility but to the universal human desire for good, which is the center and basis for a sense of the dignity and significance of every human life.

Suggested Reading:

Coles, *Simone Weil.*

Weil, *The Need for Roots.*

————, *Selected Essays.*

Questions to Consider:

1. Compare Weil's conception of justice to the principles of other figures we have studied thus far.

2. Weil characterizes her essay "Draft from a Statement of Human Obligations" as a "profession of faith." How does her view of faith differ from Kierkegaard's?

Lecture Thirty—Transcript
Simone Weil—Imagining the Secular Saint

With this lecture, we now begin the final section of our course by formally introducing the conception of the secular saint as the figure who we propose embodies the experience of the human search for meaning in the historical context of the second half of the 20th century and the beginning of the 21st century. With the introduction of the secular saint, we're in a certain way breaking new ground, both in the course and, to some extent, in cultural discourse. It's a new idea that asks us to look at human existence and its search for meaning as a question and a commitment in what I think is a distinctively new way. First, we'll try to offer a purely conceptual attempt to define the figure of the secular saint as a metaphor, and then go about trying to put some flesh and blood on those bare conceptual bones, first by examining the identity of Simone Weil— whom we've already encountered in an earlier lecture—further because of my conviction at least that she embodies this ideal type (the secular saint) as closely as is humanly possible; and then go on to add other examples and perspectives in subsequent lectures.

We can characterize the secular saint as an ideal type of person who lives the question of meaning in human existence fully open to its mystery and fully committed to searching for meaning along the paths of both the hero and the saint. We have to acknowledge that as we have presented these two paths and their historical development through Western culture, they are, in a fundamental sense, really mutually exclusive opposites that resist synthesis or assimilation. To use Kuhn's term, they are incommensurable ways of experiencing reality, so that the figure of the secular saint—which we said a moment ago lives both pathways of experience—has to appear to us at first and remain a paradox and a question: What could it possibly mean to live life fully open to and in pursuit of meaning in human existence along both paths simultaneously in the course of one human experience? This paradoxical character makes the figure of the secular saint a kind of embodiment and affirmation of the human person primarily in terms of his or her freedom of conscience exercised as an absolute responsibility for one's identity in relation to the mystery of reality as a whole.

Identifying the secular saint in terms of freedom and responsibility for the meaning of one's existence through a choice, a series of choices, that could always genuinely and authentically be made otherwise, carries the important consequence that such choices can never be made once and for all, as we saw Frankl point out in our last lecture. The images that we use to characterize the way of living of the secular saint will be two metaphors: binocularity, that is the necessity of seeing from two distinct perspectives simultaneously to allow depth of field; the second metaphoric image we'll use is the phenomenon of walking erect as an evolutionary stage of human development requiring the capacity—in order to walk two feet rather than four—to balance constant shifts of weight and momentum; a movement of opposites, contradictory shifts of one's place in the world, one's stance in the world, and yet something that, over millennia of evolution, human beings learned to do. This raises an important issue about the comparison of biological evolution to cultural evolution to the evolution of identity in an individual human life, and the recognition that we're talking about significantly different timeframes here. Fortunately, they're functioning each for us metaphorically, so we don't have to worry about figuring out precisely what the relationship is.

Simone Weil, as our first example of the identity, the profile of the secular saint, has been widely regarded as a creative genius by figures as diverse as Albert Camus, T. S. Eliot, Paul Tillich, Hannah Arendt, Dorothy Day, Robert Coles, and even Charles de Gaulle, who in addition to considering her a genius thought she was crazy. Weil was born in Paris in 1909; she died at the age of 34 in a sanatorium in Kent, England, of tuberculosis significantly complicated by her refusal of food to demonstrate solidarity with those of her countrymen in Nazi-occupied France whom she longed to join as an active member of the Resistance. Her parents were non-religious Jews; her brother André became one of the most illustrious mathematicians of the 20th century. Throughout her life, she suffered from a weak constitution and severe physical ailments, especially chronic debilitating headaches. She was born both physically and socially awkward and her personality developed a ruthless strain of self-criticism. Let me read you something from one of her essays about her early experience:

> At fourteen I fell into one of those fits of bottomless despair that comes with adolescence, and I seriously thought of dying because of the mediocrity of my natural faculties. The exceptional gifts of my brother, who had a childhood and

youth comparable to those of Pascal, brought my own inferiority home to me. I did not mind having no visible successes, but what did grieve me was the idea of being excluded from that transcendent kingdom to which only the truly great have access and wherein truth abides. I prepared to die rather than to live without that truth. After months of inward darkness, I suddenly had the everlasting conviction that any human being, even though practically devoid of natural faculties, can penetrate to the kingdom of truth reserved for genius, if only he longs for truth and perpetually concentrates all his attention upon its attainment. ... The conviction that had come to me was that when one hungers for bread one does not receive stones.

Despite her low assessment of her own intellectual abilities, she had brilliant academic successes and achievements; and although they attracted a great deal of attention, she pursued a career teaching Greek philosophy in a secondary school for girls in rural France. Her brief life was bracketed by the two World Wars and shaped by the political, social, and economic dislocations that dominated the years between the two wars. In her life, she registered the anguish of her times with exquisite and painful sensitivity, and felt obligated to rethink Europe's collapsing civilization. In the 1930s, she was active on the political left, immersing herself in trade union politics and worker education. She left teaching for a year to experience life as a factory worker; her descriptions of those times are extraordinarily vivid. They portray the workers' existence in terms that would make Marx's mustache curl. She left teaching again to fight fascism in the Spanish Civil War until an accident forced her to return to France. Albert Camus called her essays of this period the most penetrating and prophetic contributions to Western political and social thought since Marx. In the last five years of her life, short as it was, a kind of mystical spiritual perspective opened to her in a completely unexpected way. She came, she said, to know the love of God as intimately as the smile of a friend. We'll examine her religious thought and her spiritual experience in the next lecture.

Weil's thoughts on the political and economic dynamics of society, which will be our concern in the rest of this lecture, have their roots primarily in Greek philosophy, and most especially in the thought of Plato, and they reflect the characteristics of the heroic worldview and the concept of heroic citizenship that evolved from it as we've detailed it in previous lectures. As with Plato, justice was the question that shaped and guided all of her political as well as philosophical concerns. Weil's conception of justice is absolutely simple and perfectly straightforward: Justice, she says, consists in seeing that no avoidable harm is done to any person. As I said, its simplicity is striking; it's, in one sense, absolutely minimal—simply do no harm and avoid harm being done—and yet what it takes to accomplish that goal opens for Weil onto a moral and political vision that is stunning in the literal sense of the word: it stops us cold in our tracks; we'll try to elaborate on that a little further.

They understand human existence as a whole, and questions of justice specifically, in the context of the impersonal worldview of Greek philosophy. She articulates this vision most clearly in one of her very last works, the essay "Draft from a Statement of Human Obligations," which she wrote as a sort of executive summary of the only complete book that she wrote during her life, entitled *The Need for Roots*. It was this executive summary when it was passed on to de Gaulle that evoked the comment I made earlier. He was horrified that a suggestion about how to establish, to rebuild, French society and establish justice within that society could fly so directly and flagrantly in the face of what from even the most legitimate point of view would have to be referred to as realpolitik. Completely unrealistic; she's crazy, he thought.

Weil designates her essay "Draft from a Statement of Human Obligations"—designates it right at the beginning as a superscript to the essay—a "profession of faith." I'm sure this is one of the reasons why Camus recognized in her a kindred spirit; there's no argument here that we're getting at the truth, there's no argument here that this view of justice is based on an accurate perception of reality and the order of reality in such a way that the conclusions that she will draw follow methodologically from those initial premises. This is a choice like Kierkegaard's leap into the abyss, and she labels it as such. This is the voice of freedom speaking an act of faith.

The essay's worldview, like that of Plato's philosophy, is divided into the separate realms of body and of soul. The realm of the body—the world of time, space, and material existence—is ruled by the force of necessity, and in it, humans are absolutely subjected to the misery of need. The realm of the soul, on the other hand, is governed by the creative energy that exists outside space and time.

Although this reality is mysterious and beyond the comprehension of intellect and beyond the reach of the will, it corresponds to the universal human desire for an absolute good, which Weil insisted is at the bottom of the heart of every person. For Weil, this desire is the reality of the soul itself, so that her conception of the soul is—it's important to notice, I think—fundamentally erotic in the strict etymological sense of the word; it's a conception of good as correlative to a yearning, a passionate desire at the bottom of the human heart; a longing and leaning outward toward the beauty of the good itself. This corresponds, again, closely to the conception of reality, the mythic image of the soul's journey to reality that we find in Plato; for example, the vision of the good that we found at the center of the allegory of the cave in *The Republic*.

Weil goes on to say that the only possible link between the two realms of body and soul is human freedom; the capacity every person always has to consent or withhold consent in the directing of their attention beyond the world of matter, space, and time to that transcendent good that is shared by all in terms of desire; that transcendent good that alone can wholly satisfy the fullest desire of the human heart. Let's reflect on that for just a second. What she's saying seems to be something like this: In the reality of human existence in the body—that is, in our forlorn condition as biological creatures in space and time—we experience a longing that could only be satisfied by something that did not exist within the limits of space, time, and matter. Her argument is simply that something transcendent, that absolute good, must exist; otherwise human existence—specifically that existence, that erotic impulse, that desire for an absolute good—would be altogether absurd, and Weil does not believe that human existence is altogether absurd. It is genuinely absurd, but it is also—here's the structure of the personality we're identifying as the secular saint—human existence is genuinely absurd, that's reality. Human existence is also meaningful on a basis of the desire that everyone experiences, and therefore could not fail but to be fulfilled. The reason for that is precisely the secret that Weil points to in her life, and that we want to try to explore.

Going back to her development in the essay, this notion of consent as the fundamental act of freedom—consenting to attend, to pay attention, to look for, to search—this consent to attend to the good is the only possible path of entry, Weil thinks, into the world of truth, justice, and beauty; meanings and values by which humans live.

Apart from this link, between the transcendent good and the consenting soul, human existence in the material world is, as we've said, entirely subject to the totalitarian force of oppression; a force that renders experience in its face absurd.

Weil's conception of justice is based on a notion of obligation, the strictest form of obligation: the obligation of every person to do all in his or her power to avoid harm being done to human beings; to meet the needs of both body and soul of every human being. In other words, the notion of obligation is the pivot on which Weil's idea of justice turns, because it is the expression of—as she puts it—absolute respect for that desire for transcendent good in the soul which is the heart of every person. She regards this desire as sacred and inviolable because it alone is the source of all possible meaning and all possible value in human experience. Respect for the universal desire for a total good cannot, she says, be shown directly; it's not tangible, it's not a fact. On the other hand, unless it's enacted, it's meaningless, this respect. Weil claims that respect can be shown indirectly by demonstrating that respect for those needs that human beings suffer as a result of their forlorn condition of exposure to the force of necessity. She puts it this way:

> The link which attaches the human being to the reality outside the world is, like the reality itself, beyond the reach of human faculties. The respect that it inspires as soon as it is recognized cannot be expressed to it.
>
> This respect cannot, in this world, find any form of direct expression. But unless it is expressed it has no existence. There is a possibility of indirect expression for it.
>
> The respect inspired by the link between man and the reality outside the world can be expressed to that part of man which exists in the reality of this world.
>
> The reality of this world is necessity. The part of man which is in this world is the part which is in bondage to necessity and subject to the misery of need.
>
> The one possibility of indirect expression of respect for the human being is offered by men's needs, the needs of the soul and of the body, in this world.

She goes on to say that the needs of the body are food, shelter, clothing, and physical security. The needs of the soul are meaning and value, rooted in freedom of conscience. The soul hungers and thirsts for meaning, value, and a sense of identity, just as the body hungers and thirsts for food and drink. Hence, Weil says, the whole person, body and soul, thirsts for justice; that is, that no harm be done to what is sacred in any person. Weil distinguishes sharply between human needs on the one hand, and preferential desires, even legitimate rights, on the other hand. There are some things that all human beings genuinely need; they cannot be human without them. Food is one, meaning another. There are many things that individuals desire more or less; these desires are preferential. She makes it completely clear that no one has any obligation to fulfill the preferential wishes of another person; on the other hand, she says, everyone has an absolute obligation to meet the genuine needs of any other human being, without qualification. Frankly, this is precisely what de Gaulle thought was crazy. The idea that quite literally everything had to stop anytime we encounter a human being who is suffering deprivation of something that they genuinely need to be human; we hear the echo here in a very different context of the Sartrean notion of total responsibility, conceived—in the case of Sartre, obviously—without the notional of obligation. But it's precisely this notion in Weil that puts her in the position that we're terming or we're identifying with that of the secular saint.

Weis uses the term "affliction" to designate an intensity of suffering, whether naturally or deliberately caused, which does harm not only to personal sensibility—to one's feelings, to one's body; as important as that is—but also does harm to the universal human desire for good, which is the soul, the center, and basis for the sense of the dignity and significance of every human life. Because affliction thus mutilates and humiliates, dehumanizes the sufferer until it annihilates the hope that good can be done to them, affliction imposes—she believes—an unconditional obligation on all human beings to do all that is within their power to alleviate it; or failing that, to demonstrate their compassion in a way that makes the sufferer realize that he or she is not alone in his or her affliction.

Weis says, with regard to the notion of affliction:

> Because of it, when a man's life is destroyed or damaged by some wound or privation of soul or body, which is due to

other men's actions or negligence, it is not only his sensibility that suffers but also his aspiration towards the good. Therefore there has been sacrilege towards that which is sacred in him

This notion of justice, specified through her conception of absolute obligation, an obligation that is outside the realm of barter and exchange, outside the realm of any calculus of realpolitik, of comparative advantage and disadvantage, outside the realm of negotiation. This conception of absolute obligation is what she perceived to be the absolute necessity in order for the search for meaning and value—in her conception social justice—to be pursued by human beings. We'd have to explore it in much greater detail to refute—which I think is both possible and necessary—de Gaulle's judgment on her political vision that it's crazy. But the difficultly of that, and the legitimation to some extent of de Gaulle's point of view, we catch a glimpse of in recognition that this draft of a statement of human obligation precedes by just about six years the United Nations Charter of Universal Human Rights, and we notice how different the two conceptions of justice are. For Weil, justice is impossible without the recognition of obligations which nothing, including national sovereignty of nations and the international rule of law, can fail to recognize.

We know that the realpolitik of the draft statement of universal human rights finally in the end had to acquiesce to the ultimacy of national sovereignty as a norm that could not be overridden. Weil's vision of justice leaves us with the question: If we hunger and thirst for justice in our time and in our place, how is it to be found?

Lecture Thirty-One
Simone Weil—A New Augustine?

Scope:

This lecture examines Simone Weil's religious sensibility and writings through a parallel of comparison and contrast with saint Augustine. Both figures stand at the cultural and personal intersection of classical secular humanism and scriptural religion. They both struggle to respond to the claims of human truths they found in each of these traditions and to mediate the values of both to their contemporaries. But the differences between them in this shared pivotal role are equally telling: Augustine chose to interrelate the two cultures and traditions through the process of conversion; Weil passionately refused to accept conversion because it meant giving up the reality of one ideal for the sake of the other. In so doing she made herself a paradigmatic figure of the 20th century. She appears as a hero without the hope of justice, and a saint without the sustaining bonds of religious community. The tension which her life embodies brings into focus the question of forgiveness at the center of the contemporary search for meaning: Can the impossibility of wholeness which human death both symbolizes and seals be authentically and freely affirmed as the meaning of life?

Outline

I. In this lecture we examine the saintly dimension of Simone Weil's extraordinary identity.

II. Like Saint Augustine, Weil experienced her whole life as a search for the truth of reality as whole; the truth of that transcendent mystery beyond time, space, and matter, which shone with the radiance of perfect beauty and overpowered the heart with unquenchable desire.

    A. As we have seen, memories of her own childhood held premonitions of the secret she discovered and lived in the last five years of her life.

B. It was not until she was motivated to read the Christian Gospels, prompted by the simplicity of faith of many of the works she taught and a few humane and intelligent clergy and friends, that she gradually came to discover what she had been searching for all her life.

III. Simone Weil completely rejects the dynamics of conversion and with it any dream of "catholicity" as universalization of the culture of faith in the secular order of society.

    A. Weil refused personal conversion to Catholicism and would not accept baptism despite her recognition that she had lived her whole life in the spirit that she discovered in her reading of the Christian Gospels.

    B. Weil explained her reason for refusing conversion in terms of the demands of love.

    C. She further explains that what frightened her about the Catholic Church, and by extension all other forms of organized religion, was that as institutions they necessarily fell subject to the forces of collectivism.

IV. Weil's situation, caught between the universality of justice and the personal intimacy of love, is a powerful example of what we have termed the "forlorn" condition of existence in context of a world dominated by totalitarian forces.

    A. Weil heroically refused to prioritize the truth of a personal existence enlightened by love at the expense of the universality of justice.

    B. Weil's personality is undoubtedly most characterized by the extremism of her uncompromising demands on herself and others which produced a profound physical, psychological, and spiritual burden that many have noted and some have harshly criticized.

    C. On the other hand, many claim to recognize a saint for the modern age based on Weil's willingness to forego the consolations of religious faith in order to keep faith and solidarity with the poor, all those to whom she believed she had an obligation to show respect because they suffered the misery of affliction.

Suggested Reading:

"Enlightened by Love."

Weil, *Gravity and Grace.*

———, *Waiting for God.*

Questions to Consider:

1. Weil's situation of herself as somehow in between Judaism and Catholicism, yet formally committed to neither, leads us to think about the relationship between the figure of the saint and religion. How have other saintly figures responded to institutionalized religion?

2. Similarly, Weil, despite her mystical tendencies, was firmly rooted in the context of contemporary politics and social issues, fighting fascism in the Spanish Civil War and working in a factory. How has the saint's relationship to society changed and evolved since the figures from the beginning of our course?

Lecture Thirty-One—Transcript
Simone Weil—A New Augustine?

In this lecture, we're going to continue the examination of Simone Weil's life as the substance for our initial sketch of the identity of the secular saint. In the last lecture, we examined the heroic profile of Weil's identity. In this lecture, we're going to continue our study of Weil with a focus on the saintly dimension of Weil's extraordinary identity. Recall that the conception of the secular saint, which we're developing, depends on the creative energy flowing between two poles of human identity—the personal and the impersonal, the saintly and the heroic—and the two distinct pathways along which the hero and the saint travel in their search for human meaning. Like the force field that sustains an electrical current and is capable of generating light, the capacity of each pathway to lead to meaningful human experience is short-circuited if the two poles collapse into one another; they have to remain separated and yet joined by the tension between them to be effective. We have identified this structure of unity amid difference as the structure of both human freedom and its inherent ambiguity and, also, that potential for meaning that is the structural reality of metaphor. This polarity in both cases—the ambiguity of freedom, the possibility of a yes and a no, the structure of metaphor, both same and different, and both familiar and strange—generates the light that we call meaning.

Simone Weil's religious identity is as intensely and intimately personal as that of any religious mystic, even such rapturous visionaries as Saint Catherine of Siena or Saint Teresa of Avila. Yet, she distanced herself from her Jewish heritage, and she adamantly refused to be baptized a Christian. Our goal in this lecture is to observe how the incandescent light of Weil's humanity radiated the energy that arose in her life from the tension between a hunger and thirst for justice and a passionate yearning for intimacy with the beauty of divine truth which she so longed for throughout her life, and which she said has the capacity to enlighten the mind and fill the heart with love.

Like Saint Augustine, Weil experienced her whole life as a search for the truth of reality as a whole; the truth of that transcendent mystery beyond time, space, and matter, which shone with the radiance of perfect beauty and overpowered the heart with unquenchable desire. In her final years, Weil came to believe, like Saint Augustine, that the beauty of truth for which the heart so yearns could be addressed as a beloved person whose smile of recognition held the secret meaning of a human being's existence. As we've seen, memories of her own childhood held for Weil premonitions of the secret she discovered and lived only in the last five or so years of her life. It wasn't until she was motivated to read the Christian Gospels, prompted by the simplicity of faith of many of the workers she taught and also a few humane and intelligent clergy and friends. It wasn't until then that she gradually came to discover what she had been searching for all her life, not precisely in Christianity, but in a certain experience of human intimacy; that "I-thou" relationship that Buber spoke of, but expressed not so much in terms of conversation, but in terms of this image of a smile of recognition.

She connects that discovery with the strange story of how she came to be familiar with a poem of George Herbert's. She says in her book *Waiting for God*:

> I discovered a poem. … It is called "Love." I learned it by heart. Often, at the culminating point of a violent headache, I make myself say it over, concentrating all my attention upon it and clinging with all my soul to the tenderness it enshrines. I used to think I was merely reciting it as a beautiful poem, but without my knowing it the recitation had the virtue of a prayer. It was during one of these recitations that, as I told you, Christ himself came down and took possession of me. … Moreover, in this sudden possession of me by Christ, neither my senses nor my imagination had any part; I only felt in the midst of my suffering the presence of a love, like that which one can read in the smile on a beloved face.

Let me read to you now the poem to which she's referring by George Herbert. It is, as she said, entitled "Love."

> Love bade me welcome, yet my soul drew back,
> Guilty of dust and sin.
> But quick-ey'd Love, observing me grow slack
> From my first entrance in,
> Drew nearer to me, sweetly questioning
> If I lack'd anything.

"A guest, "I answer'd, "worthy to be here;"
Love said, "You shall be he."
"I, the unkind, the ungrateful? ah my dear,
I cannot look on thee."
Love took my hand and smiling did reply,
"Who made the eyes but I?"

"Truth, Lord, but I have marr'd them; let my shame
Go where it doth deserve."
"And know you not," says Love, "who bore the blame?"
"My dear, then I will serve."
"You must sit down," says Love, "and taste my meat." So I
did sit and eat.

This extraordinary experience of a genuine mystical transport that they'd described as occasioned by the words of this poem have profound significance for the particular sensibility of her religious spirituality, religious without a religion; an experience of that person-to-person intimacy, of that particular dimension of love that we saw established at the very origin of the religions of the book: with Abraham; the Covenant relationship. In Weil's case, it is sealed Eucharistically; that is, with a shared meal, rather than sacrificially. We'll return to this later to develop its significance further. We should note, therefore, in this experience of Weil, her proximity to the saintly paradigm not only of Saint Augustine but also of Saint Francis of Assisi, and also of Francis's devoted scribe, Dante, who makes the smile of the beloved—the smile of Beatrice—the very signature of Divine love.

Unlike Saint Augustine, Simone Weil completely rejects the dynamism of conversion, and with it any dream of "catholicity" that universalism and universalization of the culture of faith into the realm of secular society and its natural order. In this most particularly, Weil exemplifies the sense in which we are proposing the metaphor of the "secular saint" as particularly appropriate to our own cultural and existential situation. We've mentioned that Weil refused personal conversion to Catholicism despite her enchantment with the Christian Gospels; and would not accept baptism despite her recognition that as she says in many different ways, she had lived her whole life in the spirit she discovered in her reading of the scriptures. She says that the gospel spirit of poverty had been alive in her from her earliest childhood memory; that she had fallen in love with Saint

Francis of Assisi as soon as she had come to know of him. She says further that she had been obsessed by the scriptural idea of love of neighbor since childhood, although she had called it by the name of justice. Again, she says she learned from Marcus Aerelius the Stoic conception of amor fati, which she had come to understand later as obedience to the will of God. Weil explained her reason for refusing conversion in terms of what she took to be the obligations of love. She says again in *Waiting for God*:

> Christianity should contain all vocations without exception since it is catholic. In consequence the Church should also. But in my eyes Christianity is catholic by right but not in fact. So many things are outside it, so many things that God loves, otherwise they would not be in existence.

She further explains that what frightened her about the Catholic Church, and by extension all other forms of organized religion, was that as institutions they necessarily fell subject to the forces of collectivism and totalitarianism. She was perfectly well aware that institutionalization is a necessary structure of any human culture; without structure, nothing can exist in the world of space and time. As a social structure, however, human cultures—including religious cultures—are ultimately subject to the laws of cause and effect that govern all matter, psychological and social matter, as well as physical. The subjection by institutional religion of the human spirit, of the desire for pure good, to these forces of institutionalization— she believes—is a form of oppression and a cause of spiritual suffering that either produces human misery by separating people from the whole truth and from one another, or causes the deformity of spirit that she called "church patriotism." For Weil, "church patriotism" is a metaphor that she uses to distinguish a partialization of the whole truth of a basic human need: Humans needed both rootedness in a local culture with which they are able to identify and live familiarly in concrete experiential ways, and, at the same time, humans need to participate in forms of community that are universal and transcend the strictures of any particular homeland. The overemphasis of the first of these counterpointal needs, she says, is bigotry; the overemphasis of the second is totalitarianism.

We have here, again, another image of this notion of the stabilizing tension; a kind of balance between opposites. Although we have two genuine needs, an overemphasis on the fulfillment of one destabilizes and imbalances the fulfillment of the other. Weil's personal situation, the situation that she envisions herself sharing with all human beings, caught between the universality of justice and the personal intimacy of love, is—it seems to me—a extraordinarily powerful example of what we have termed the "forlorn" condition of human existence in the context of a world dominated by forces of totalization. It's the no-man's land, upon which the drama of World War I unfolded. Her way of living the question of meaning posed by that situation—of being forlorn; of being alone in no-man's land—and her commitment to search for integrity of identity in the truth of reality as a whole exemplifies what we're trying to characterize with the metaphor of the secular saint. "Faith [she says] is the experience that the intelligence is lighted up by love. The organ in us through which we see truth is the intelligence; the organ in us through which we see God is love."

As we've said, Weil heroically refused to prioritize the truth of a personal vision and a personal experience enlightened by love at the expense of the universality of justice; she would not separate herself from those who were marginalized or excluded by any social institution, including the church that claimed to be the sanctuary of the gospel message that she found so beautiful. Weil puts it this way: "I should betray the truth, that is to say the aspect of truth that I see, if I left the point, where I have been since my birth, at the intersection of Christianity and everything that is not Christianity."

That is the situation expressed in terms of Weil's own individual, personal experience; but that point she will not give up is the intersection that identifies the place of the secular Saint. Simone Weil's personality is undoubtedly most characterized by the extremism of her uncompromising demands on herself and others which produced a profound physical, psychological, and spiritual burden that she struggled under for her whole life; and which many have noted and some have—with some legitimacy—harshly criticized. Harvard psychiatrist Robert Coles, in a very valuable book on they, explores microscopically those tendencies toward extremism in Weil's personality; recognizing them for what they were—profound human limitations and sufferings—and yet at the same time identifying in them a creative spark that was the fuel of both the light and the heat of Weil's passionate intellect.

On the other hand, apart from her extremism, many who claim to recognize in her a new kind of saint for a modern age based on, or rather the basis for that claim of a saintliness in Weil's identity rests on Weil's willingness to forgo the consolations of institutional religious identification; membership in a faith community in order to keep faith and solidarity with the poor. All of those, to whom she believed she had an obligation to show respect; an absolute obligation that could not be foregone or postponed for any reason, especially personal gratification or satisfaction. She believed that the obligation was absolutely binding because those who were in need suffered the misery of affliction, especially those whose needs went unmet due to the neglect by those who profess faith in God.

Weil expresses it in a moving passage; she says:

> A beautiful thing involves no good except itself, in its totality, as it appears to us. We are drawn toward it without knowing what to ask of it. It offers us its own existence. We do not desire anything else, we possess it, and yet we still desire something. We do not in the least know what it is. We want to get behind beauty, but it is only a surface. It is like a mirror that sends us back our own desire for goodness. It is a sphinx, an enigma, a mystery which is painfully tantalizing. We should like to feed upon it but it is merely something to look at; it appears only from a certain distance. The great trouble in human life is that looking and eating are two different operations. Only beyond the sky, in the country inhabited by God, are they one and the same operation. Children feel this trouble already, when they look at a cake for a long time almost regretting that it should be that vice, depravity, and crime are nearly always, or even perhaps always, in their essence, attempts to eat beauty, to eat what we should only look at. Eve began it. If she caused humanity to be lost by eating the fruit, the opposite attitude, looking at the fruit without eating it, should be what is required to save it. "Two winged companions," says an Upanishad, "two birds are on the branch of a tree. One eats the fruit, the other looks at it." Those two birds are the two parts of our soul.

An extraordinarily striking phrase, I'm sure you'll agree. The human heart desires beauty above all else: the beauty of truth, the beauty of justice, the beauty of whatever it considers to be good. There is something absolutely natural in our biological identity: To hunger and thirst for that which we want, because it is by eating, by nutrition that we become more intimately associated with the fulfillment of our desire than in any other experience that we possess as animals. The other becomes us; it feeds us so intimately and so deeply that we become perfectly at one with it. But that intimacy, that at-one myth, requires a death; in order to be digested, the beautiful must be consumed. If our food offers itself to us, then that death is not simply in a Christian metaphor, but in one of the oldest metaphors of human religious experience: that offering of food to the one who lives by it; not by way of self-sacrifice but by way of feasting.

Go back to the image that Weil evokes through her meditation on George Herbert's poem. This sitting down together at the banquet table of God and man, of one human being with another human being, and the exchange of self as food; that exchange of self that requires a death, indeed an exchange of death, and yet gives new life. This is not poetry for her, in other words, or not simply poetry. One of the things that Robert Coles, as I mentioned, explores in his book is the long chain of evidence of a recurrent tendency at least toward anorexia, toward eating disorders, that culminates in what initially was judged by the medical coroner as her suicide by means of the hunger strike that so complicated her tuberculosis. Something profound and deeply human—deeply human because it is so deeply ambiguous—was at work in Weil, and she struggled with it for all of her life, in a sense consuming herself as the food that her spirit needed to produce the light that she sheds on the human situation, especially in the 20th century.

This ambiguity of the image of eating—Eucharistic on the one hand, murderously sacrificial on the other—is a way, I think of sensing the precarious balance that Weil had to strike in her own life that we must strike in any attempt to understand her life, but most importantly that we must struggle to maintain in our lives, in our own search for meaning, that delicate balance between murderous consumption, whether at the biological level, the economic level, the psychological level, the social level, even the religious level. The need to eat reality alive and make it our own so as to possess it, as opposed to the spirit of hospitality, which is exchanged between persons where people sit down together at a table and exchange nourishment. This delicate balance is the home; it's the proper place of the secular saint who refuses as Weil did to surrender either polarity, either aspect of the truth as they experience it, despite the irreconcilability of the conflict between the two sides.

In our remaining lectures, we're going to try to flesh out further the image of the secular saint by exploring the example of other individual human beings and reflecting on other cultural manifestations of this problem of striking a humane balance between love of other and the appropriate love of self: the path of the saint and the path of the hero.

Lecture Thirty-Two
Identifying the Secular Saint

Scope:

Without attempting to offer a fixed definition, this lecture explores further the identity of the secular saint by examining the mark made on contemporary society by two other figures who challenge the boundaries between the traditional types of hero and saint: Mother Teresa of Calcutta and Martin Luther King Jr. Although each life portrays a unique identity formed in response to significantly different societal crises, both reveal a shared urgency to address the shared human condition of affliction and vulnerability to the immediate proximity of death as the central focus of the search for meaning. Although both functioned within the mainstream of the Western scriptural religious tradition, they emphasized, each in their own way, the necessity to integrate the absolute reality of death into the very center of the human search for the meaning of life. Mother Theresa did this through her mission to uphold the dignity of the dying homeless, as did King through his advocacy of nonviolent resistance as a response to social injustice. Taken together with Simone Weil, they help identify the secular saint as the metaphor that we use to try to draw our considerations to a conclusion.

Outline

I. Although the lives of Martin Luther King Jr. and Mother Teresa clearly qualify them for inclusion in the category of saint as we are using the term, this lecture explores whether their identities might be more authentically revealed through the designation of secular saint.

    A. We propose the notion of the secular saint as a counterbalance to the violence against humanity gendered by the dynamics of totalitarianism.

    B. The point made here is not to misappropriate the motivations and identities of King and Mother Teresa, but rather, the to probe more deeply their profound contributions to the human search for meaning.

II. Martin Luther King Jr.'s famous letter from Birmingham Jail makes clear the dual sources of his inspiration and ideals: both the Christian spirit of agape, or universal love based on the love of God; and the *arete*, the heroic virtue of citizenship.

    A. As with Simone Weil, King's language makes clear that the traditions and values of both ideals, hero and saint, have been so thoroughly intertwined in the Western tradition as to be inseparable even though they are ultimately incommensurable.

    B. King appeals directly to Socrates as he does to the Gospels to explain and vindicate his course of action.

    C. At the same time, King impugns racial segregation on moral grounds, which in turn are grounded in divine law.

III. In his Nobel lecture, King articulates the necessary connection of opposition to racism with opposition to all forms of violence against humanity.

    A. King uses his own version of Plato's body-soul distinction to identify a type of poverty of spirit, which he claims is particularly characteristic of our time.

    B. His diagnosis of spiritual failure to thrive in Western culture is rooted in the dynamics of violence and oppression which he detects in the interrelation of racism with poverty and war.

    C. The practice of nonviolence and its efficacy in overcoming all forms of totalitarian violence is rooted in the heroic virtue of self-respect and self-mastery.

IV. Mother Teresa of Calcutta gained international recognition for her ministry to the poor, orphaned, sick, and dying.

    A. Mother Teresa experienced early in her religious life a series of personal revelations that convinced her it was absolutely imperative that she refuse Jesus nothing he might ask of her.

    B. Mother Teresa made it clear in everything she said and did that her purpose was not primarily to alleviate suffering but to recognize it, and thus to communicate to those suffering that they were loved by God through fellow humans.

C. She had no small number of critics who charged that her priorities were misplaced, that by not working for justice as King did, by not militating for a change of conscience and of institutions, the consolation she offered was merely palliative, not curative of the disease.

D. Interiorly, however, Mother Teresa lived immersed in spiritual darkness.

E. Only in her ministry to the poor, especially the dying, did Teresa experience her existence as meaningful.

F. Teresa is the opposite of Weil: outside a saint, within a hero; through recognition she made of death not simply a friend but a divine lover.

V. The common theme uniting Mother Teresa and Martin Luther King is the capacity of human freedom to transcend violence and give meaning to life my making peace with death.

Suggested Reading:

King, Nobel Prize lecture.

Kolodiejchuk, *Mother Teresa*.

Mother Teresa, Nobel lecture.

Washington, *A Testament of Hope*.

Questions to Consider:

1. Were you surprised to learn about the spiritual darkness Mother Teresa experienced? Does this fit the saintly or heroic pattern? Can you think of other figures who reported similar experiences?

2. Both Martin Luther King Jr. and Mother Teresa were awarded the Nobel Peace Prize. Do you think that the Peace Prize is a way of honoring or "canonizing" secular saints? other recent recipients include Al Gore, Muhammed Yunus, Jimmy Carter, and Nelson Mandela—can these figures (and other Nobel Peace Prize recipients) be considered secular saints? Why or why not?

Lecture Thirty-Two—Transcript
Identifying the Secular Saint

Although the lives of Martin Luther King, Jr. and Mother Teresa clearly qualify them for inclusion in the category of saints as we've talked about that term, and as, of course, we understand it in everyday language, this lecture wants to explore whether their identities might not be more authentically—in a certain sense, more truthfully—revealed through the designation of secular saint. In the last lecture, we concluded our examination of Simone Weil's identity, and used her as our first concrete example of what might be the meaning of this notion of secular saint, and what might be the value of employing it as a way of addressing the unique historical situation that we find ourselves in as a culture today. Rather than simply being a matter of terminology, this suggestion of the notion of the secular saint, this question that touches on the issue of freedom as the source of meaning, and freedom as in and of itself necessarily carrying with it the reality of an ambiguity; that is, of two real possibilities, and those possibilities being necessary for the power human beings experience in and as the reality of freedom, this reality of freedom as we saw it proposed by Frankl.

We want to focus in this lecture on amplifying and further testing the notion of the secular saint as it embodies the main characteristics of an identity that, in a certain way, is forced to live in the presence of two worldviews and keep its balance; use two different points of perspective to gain a depth of field and a richness of meaning that is otherwise unavailable. The notion of the secular saint signifies, in other words, a readiness to inhabit the reality of both worldviews without excluding or privileging either. Thus we propose the notion of the secular saint as a counterbalance to the violence against humanity that pushes humanity to its extreme point of isolation and devastation; that violence that is engendered by what we have referred to as the dynamics of totalitarianism.

Martin Luther King, Jr., a Baptist clergyman, consistently and compellingly appealed to scripture and Christian theology to articulate and motivate the cause of the civil rights movement, but in his emphasis on the dignity of the person as citizen as well as child of God, and in his dedication to nonviolence, I want to suggest that he showed himself committed equally to the reality of the heroic worldview. Similarly, Mother Teresa dedicated herself to embodying a love of the poor and care for their physical needs as a way of demonstrating that love. Her particular ministry of special attention to the dying arose from a concern that their deaths be recognized and shared with at least one other human being. Recognition of death as the ultimate basis of human solidarity is a value that the hero shares fully with the saint, while giving it an entirely different meaning and significance. In both cases, the being point made here is not that we want to appropriate in an unjustified way the experience, the motivations, the identities of King or Mother Teresa as they experienced themselves, as they thought about what they're doing; and by a process of kind of revisionist history and interpretation turn that into something other. Rather, the hope is to probe more deeply their profound contributions to the human search for meaning in its fullest possibilities and its particular timeliness in our present situation. In a sense, to imagine more of the reality of their identity, perhaps even than they understood.

Martin Luther King, Jr.'s famous letter from the Birmingham Jail makes clear the dual sources of his inspirations and his ideals: both the Christian spirit of agape, or universal love based on the love of God, and the heroic notion of *arete*, the virtue of citizenship. As with Simone Weil, King's language makes clear that the traditions and values of both ideals—hero and saint—have been so thoroughly intertwined in the Western tradition as to be inseparable, even though, as we have suggested in previous lectures, they are in a fundamental sense ultimately incommensurable; the hero and the saint speak different languages, which can be to a significant extent translated from one to the other, but the lived texture and reality of the experience cannot be so fully translated.

King appeals as directly to Socrates as he does to the Christian Gospels to explain and vindicate his course of action. The origin and goal, for example, of the civil rights movement in his view is justice, the right relationship among persons who are bound together by citizenship under the rule of law. King expresses it this way: "Injustice anywhere is a threat to justice everywhere. We are caught in an inescapable network of mutuality, tied in a single garment of destiny. Whatever affects one directly affects all indirectly."

What I'd like to point out is that this statement, the idea it expresses, can be perfectly, appropriately understood as coming directly, and indeed solely, from the vision of the Platonic Socrates as it's expressed in the allegory of the cave in *The Republic* that we looked at in an earlier lecture. The idea of the one overriding universal good toward which all human beings aspire and strive; a good that is impersonal precisely in the sense that it is genuinely the same for all, despite differences of perception, of understanding, and of naming. King identifies the strategy of civil disobedience—which was at the heart of his leadership in the civil rights movement—with Socrates' mission as a gadfly to the Athenian conscience. At the same time, King impugns racial segregation on moral grounds, which in turn are grounded in divine law. In other words, there are two distinct sources of the single condemnation of racism that King makes. Again turning to the letter from the Birmingham jail; in King's words:

> To put it in the terms of Saint Thomas Aquinas, an unjust law is a human law that is not rooted in eternal or natural law. Any law that uplifts human personality is just. Any law that degrades human personality is unjust. All segregation statutes are unjust because segregation distorts the soul and damages the personality. It gives the segregator a false sense of superiority, and the segregated a false sense of inferiority. To use the words of Martin Buber, the great Jewish philosopher, segregation substitutes an "I-it" relationship for the "I-thou" relationship, and ends up relegating persons to the status of things. So segregation is not only politically, economically and sociologically unsound, but it is morally wrong and sinful. Paul Tillich has said that sin is separation. Isn't segregation and essential expression of man's tragic separation, an expression of his awful estrangement, his terrible sinfulness?

We want to note in that statement of King's that I just read how comfortable he is—here's our first major piece of evidence for the claim that King should be understood as a secular saint—how easily he moves back and forth between two different language traditions: Segregation is both injustice, a crime against the humanity of all those who are involved, and it is a sin. You can see it both ways; you need to see it both ways. That doesn't mean we need to personally identify either with King or with anyone else; it doesn't mean we both have to be believers and theists and atheists, that's not possible. The key here I think is to remind ourselves of the nature of metaphor, and to treat all claims of ideals, all claims of meaning, all claims of value as possessing their truth metaphorically. In the metaphor, in the saint, in the hero, in the secular saint, we both see ourselves and recognize the difference between us. It doesn't matter whether you speak the language of theism, or you speak the language of I won't say atheism here but secular humanism, what matters is that you recognize the truth that each view expresses and learn to live it.

In his Nobel lecture—when he received the Nobel Peace Prize—King articulates the necessary connection of opposition to racism with opposition to all forms of violence against humanity; again, an indication of the metaphoric range of the point and the truth that King stands for. Similarly, he emphasizes the inseparability of nonviolent resistance as an instrument of change with the promotion of peace. King uses his own version of Plato's body-soul distinction to identify a type of poverty of spirit that he claims is particularly characteristic of our times. Let me read a passage from that Nobel Prize acceptance speech, in which King says:

> There is a sort of poverty of spirit which stands in glaring contrast to our scientific and technological abundance. The richer we become materially, the poorer we have become morally and spiritually. ... Our problem today is that we have allowed the internal to become lost in the external. We have allowed the means by which we live to outdistance the ends for which we live.

In that statement, I think, King is drawing our attention to an aspect of this notion of the identity of the secular saint that I would like to emphasize at this particular point, and that is the universal necessity in human living as a fundamental aspect of the search for meaning; the fundamental necessity that every human being have and live a personal spirituality. That spirituality may or may not be derived from and be practiced within something that we would recognize as an historical religious tradition and community of practice. Spirituality operates at a level of human existence and human experience prior to the level of recognizable and institutional religion, whether it includes God or not. That spirituality, that experience that as King said is the experience of the inner self, the self of meaning rather than physical and material situation, it is impossible to resist the violence of our material situation, especially to resist it nonviolently without deep wells and resources of spirituality upon which a person can call, whether or not those come from a specific religious tradition.

King's diagnosis of this spiritual failure to thrive in Western culture is rooted in the dynamics of violence and oppression which he detects in the interrelation of racism with poverty and war. He expands in the Nobel speech, in other words, the range of his concern, taking the lessons learned and the victories won within the Civil Rights movement—especially in the United States—and extending them more generally as a path of opposition, a pathway in the search for meaning within the context of the ever-expanding totalitarian forces of violence that our century exposes us to. He points out that although colonialism was eradicated for the most part by the two World Wars and their immediate aftermath, the dynamic of exploitation of natural and human resources has continued under the guise of the imbalance between developed and underdeveloped nations. War, obviously, is overt violence, but as King points out, in the past, war could be viewed as a justified means to the constructive end of opposing evil. King contends, however, in the Nobel speech that with the arrival of nuclear weapons it's become clear that war is obsolete as a credible means to achieve justice and peace. The practice of nonviolence and its efficacy in overcoming all forms of totalitarian violence is rooted in the heroic virtue of self-respect and self-mastery, as both King and Gandhi taught it. The strategy of nonviolence, in other words, depends on the human capacity to encounter death with courage born and self-possession born of the desire to excel, the desire to affirm the meaningfulness of human existence as free; a desire to do justice to freedom in oneself, equally in others, as a value in itself that requires no justification beyond itself. Again we return to Plato in *The Republic* where he argues that justice must be and can be its own reward: King the saint must be understood as being equally King the hero. One final quotation from King's Nobel acceptance speech; he says:

> I believe in this method because I think it is the only way to reestablish a broken community. It is the method which seeks to implement the just law by appealing to the conscience of the great decent majority who through blindness, fear, pride, and irrationality have allowed their consciences to sleep. ... There is no deficit in human resources; the deficit is in human will. ... Just as nonviolence exposed the ugliness of racial injustice, so must the infection and sickness of poverty be exposed and healed—not only its symptoms but its basic causes.

Let's turn to our second example now of this notion of the secular saint: Mother Teresa of Calcutta, an Albanian-born Roman Catholic nun, gained international recognition for her ministry to the poor, the orphaned, the sick, and the dying. Founder of the Missionaries of Charity, she initiated a movement that sought first and foremost to ensure that human need—human need in the sense we saw Simone Weil articulate it—did not, at the least, go unrecognized. Notice the congruence here between Weil's notion of justice and Mother Teresa's notion of charity. For Weil, the important thing for justice is at least do no harm; for Mother Teresa, at least if you cannot alleviate suffering and death recognize it. Like Martin Luther King, Mother Teresa won a Nobel Peace Prize in 1979. King was as much a hero of citizenship as he was a saint of love. In the case of Mother Teresa, her saintly identity was centered explicitly and entirely on a person-to-person relationship of intimacy; intimacy between herself and her God in the person of Jesus as the crucified lover of humanity.

Mother Teresa experienced early in her religious life a series of personal revelations that convinced her that it was absolutely imperative that she refuse Jesus nothing that he might ask of her. This phrase is repeated over and over and over again in her letters and her journals: "I want to hold nothing back; I can refuse him nothing." In order to ensure her total availability to her God, she decided that it was necessary to leave her first religious community, the Sisters of Loreto, and her duties as a teacher to minister to the poorest outcasts of Calcutta. Mother Teresa made it clear in everything she said and did that her purpose was not primarily to alleviate suffering but to recognize it—to recognize it with a human face, to acknowledge it in a human face—and thus to communicate to those who suffered and died that they were loved by God through their fellow human beings. She had no small number of critics who charged that her priorities were misplaced; basically a form of the Marxian argument "religion is the opium of the people." The charge was that by not working for justice in society as King had, by not militating for a change of conscience and of institutions, the consolation she offered was merely palliative, not curative of the disease.

The particular character, it seems to me, of Mother Teresa's spiritual genius seems to lie in its polar opposition—not conflict, but the extremity of difference—between her genius and that of Simone Weil. Weil lived consciously in a reality that to her was ruled by the absolute necessity of impersonal force; that's the way she saw the world.

Recognition of the misery of human need took the form of a respect expressed through the fulfillment of obligation to meet human needs absolutely regardless of one's ability to do so. If one could not fulfill the need, then one had to at least effectively recognize the need. Her experience of God's love was entirely separate—it was purely interior and personal, an experience in her life—from the institutions and structures of society and community. For her, institutionalization was itself a part, a partial cause, of human misery. Mother Teresa, on the other hand, worked entirely within the social dimensions of reality. She was completely identified with and obedient to the hierarchical, doctrinal, and ministerial structures of the Catholic Church. The consolation that she offered the poorest was solely that of God's love expressed through her love and that of her sisters. In that world, the world as she experienced it, she understood herself to be totally immersed in love.

At the same time, interiorly, Mother Teresa lived immersed in spiritual darkness. From almost the same time she began her new ministry, she reports continually in her letters over decades that she felt entirely forlorn, abandoned and shut out from Jesus's presence, excluded from the intimacy of her divine lover. Although she never lost faith or expressed doubt, within herself she experienced what mystical theology refers to as "the dark night of the soul." Quoting from one of her letters; she says:

> There is so much contradiction in my soul.—Such deep longing for God—so deep that it is painful—a suffering continual—and yet not wanted by God—repulsed—empty—no faith—no love—no zeal.—Souls hold no attraction—Heaven means nothing—to me it looks like an empty place—the thought of it means nothing to me and yet this torturing longing for God—pray for me please that I keep smiling at Him in spite of everything. For I am only His—so He has every right over to me. I am perfectly happy to be nobody ever to God.

It was only in her ministry to the poor, especially the dying, that Teresa experienced her existence as meaningful. She particularly identified with Saint Francis of Assisi and required her sisters to say his prayer that begins "Lord, make me an instrument of your peace" each day. For her, this meant reconciling the ultimate poverty, humiliation, and separation which the necessity of death imposes on every person with the universality of God's forgiving love. She says:

> As that man said whom we picked up from the drain, half eaten with worms, when we brought him to the home. I have lived like an animal in the street, but I am going to die like an angel, loved and cared for. And it was so wonderful to see the greatness of that man who could speak like that, who could die like that without blaming anybody, without cursing anybody, without comparing anything.

In one sense, Teresa is the opposite of Simone Weil: outside a saint, within a hero. She lives through the recognition she made of death as death's friend; not simply a friend, death as the body of a divine lover. A mystical visionary conception, no doubt; but nonetheless one that was lived with a passionate intensity that is unmistakable in everything she said and in everything she did.

The common theme uniting Mother Teresa and Martin Luther King—we've tried to suggest—is the capacity of human freedom to transcend violence and suffering s so as to give meaning to life by making peace with death. It's in this that we've tried to identify and sharpen just a little bit further one of the central characteristics of the metaphor of the secular saint that we're proposing: The secular saint is one who, through his or her journey—the shared human journey—in search of a meaningful way of living one's life makes peace. Mother Teresa's invocation of the prayer of Saint Francis—"Lord, make me an instrument of your peace"—noticing, in this case, that the peace is specifically and most fundamentally focused on the idea of making peace between the vitality of life and the inevitable suffering of death. We need to live death differently than we live life, but we need to live both in peace.

Lecture Thirty-Three
The Secular Saint at the Movies

Scope:

This lecture seeks to test the emergent identity of the secular saint as a focus of the popular imagination by charging its appearance in the artistic genre most characteristic of the 20th century: film. Using a variety of particularly successful films, including *Casablanca*, *Shane*, *The Godfather*, *Star Wars*, and the *Lord of the Rings*, this lecture surveys the ways film draws on isolated fragments of the secular saint archetype to pose the contemporary problematic of the search for meaning: How can life be whole when our culture's experience of it yields only images of trauma, fracture, and fragmentation?

Outline

I. The emergence of film as the characteristic genre of both art and popular culture in the 20th century offers a distinct and important perspective on the notion of the secular saint.

   A. The medium of film is uniquely characteristic of 20th–21st-century culture because of its distinctive blending of electronic technology with traditional elements of artistic imagination and expression.

   B. Film combines the imagistic richness and depth of texture of the plastic arts with the movement of music and dance.

II. We begin with a whirlwind tour of the dazzling but also bewildering diversity of images of heroes and saints with which the basic genres of film present us.

   A. The Western offers perhaps the most specific example of the distinctively American version of heroic identity as articulated in the Myth of the West.

   1. Western heroes embody the worldview of harsh, impersonal necessity and the warrior's code, "A man has to do what a man has to do."

   2. Iconic examples of this figure of the hero are found in films like *Shane* and films of director John Ford.

B. The genre of war films not only explores the traditional image of the warrior-hero in complex ways, but also registers and reinforces the infiltration of total war into contemporary consciousness and conscience.

    1. This genre of film provides a useful lens through which to bring the problematic theme of sacrifice into sharper focus.

    2. Examples of heroes "sacrificing their own lives" for comrades or for their country include Gary Cooper in *Sergeant York*, John Wayne in *Sands of Iwo Jima*, and Vietnam War films such as *Deer Hunter* and *Platoon*.

C. The genre of Biblical and classical epics offers paradigmatic evidence of the degree to which "In God We Trust" functions as coin of the realm in 20th century American public cultural values.

D. Christmas films offer another portrayal of religion and culture. The iconic film *It's a Wonderful Life* demonstrates saintly identity as a normative article of faith in popular culture, independent of explicit religious commitment.

E. The success of certain fantasy genre films such as the first *Star Wars* trilogy by George Lucas and *The Lord of the Rings* trilogy demonstrates the power of mythic heroic identity as an archetype of human cultural imagination in each of its major elements.

III. The character of Rick Blaine in *Casablanca* effectively embodies the identity of the secular saint and forces us to examine what the character tells us about the search for meaning in the popular imagination.

A. At the beginning of the movie, Rick is a kind of disillusioned saint. He has become a loner who makes a living from gambling without taking risks himself.

B. Rick has been disappointed in love and has renounced relationship as a source of meaning.

C. Rick is caught up unwillingly in events larger than him and receives a hero's call.

D. Rick discovers the truth about the enduring fidelity of love and in so doing finds the courage to sacrifice that personal relationship for a higher cause.

E. Rick ascends to the hero's Valhalla as he strides off to a "beautiful friendship" with Captain Renault.

V. The images of heroes and saints presented on the big screen document both the degree to which the figures have become blended and blurred together in the popular cultural imagination and the extent to which both of ideals need continual reaffirmation in the communal consciousness.

Suggested Reading:

Films: *Sergeant York*, *Sands of Iwo Jima*, *Shane*, *The Searchers*, *Ben Hur*, *The Ten Commandments*, *It's a Wonderful Life*, *Star Wars*, and *Casablanca*.

Questions to Consider:

1. Think of heroes portrayed in film that follow Joseph Campbell's pattern, or others which depart from it in some significant way.

2. How do non-American film genres both echo and depart from the models discussed here? Is the large-scale conflation of the heroic and saintly worldviews a particularly American problem? Why or why not?

Lecture Thirty-Three—Transcript
The Secular Saint at the Movies

As I was preparing these lectures, at a certain point I was discussing the idea of the course with a colleague whose judgment and whose skill as a teacher I respect immensely. We were talking it over and he said, "Well, this is all well and good, you've certainly done justice to the seriousness of the matter and the material; there's plenty of tragedy in there, there's plenty of absurdity, there's plenty of saintly generosity. But where's the sense of fun; where's the sense of humor? A course on the meaning of life without a sense of humor is not going to be worth the price of admission," which, as you might suspect, gave me pause. So I began to think about what all of those aspects and dimensions of life—a sense of humor, entertainment, recreation—all of these things share a characteristic, but where does it come from? What part of life, what part of the experience of human existence as a question and a commitment is at work in them? It occurred to me that perhaps one way of trying to understand something that, as we've emphasized repeatedly, is ultimately mysterious about the human situation, the human condition in our experience of living. One way of trying to understand that is through the metaphor of play; play as an expression of part of the truth of freedom. Freedom plays; freedom does what it does and is what it is for its own sake. No matter what metaphors we interpret the meaning, significance, and value of what it does, it does it and it does it freely, playfully, joyously, strongly, and passionately.

So in this lecture I propose we pause for a moment in the progress we're making now toward our final lectures; pause for a moment and my suggestion would be let's go to the movies. Let's go to the movies because in movies we have a characteristic expression in the 20th century and into the 21st century of both art and entertainment. Everybody loves the movies; in many, many ways it's become commonplace to say that they carried us through the difficult years of the Great Depression, the Second World War, and the tensions of the Cold War, and continue to have a central place, especially in Western popular culture. In considering film as the genre most characteristic both of art and popular culture in the 20th century, I want to suggest that this consideration can offer us a distinct and important perspective on the notion of the secular saint.

The medium of film, I'd like to suggest, is uniquely characteristic of the 20th and the 21st century culture because of its distinctive blending of electronic technology and traditional elements of artistic imagination and expression. Our historical study, as we've moved through this course, of the cultural evolution of the metaphors of hero and saint should have alerted us to the fact that adaptations of the either image—hero or saint—that are catalyzed by changing conditions in the cultural environment also require new media that are capable of conveying the meaning of those adaptive changes in ways that will effectively communicate and amplify their significance. The emergence of tragedy, for example, as an art form among the Greeks is a perfect illustration that different forms heroism require different media to convey their distinctive truth, their distinctive capacity to lend meaning and to assist and sustain the human search for meaning in new situations. Another example: Just as the exploitation of technological advances in the medium of fresco painting in the 14th and 15th century Italian Renaissance produced a vehicle—a new technology if you will; a new medium— ideally suited to the widespread dissemination of great humanistic art. Fresco painting was first and foremost a technological advance; a technological advance that made possible stylistic advances, and not only stylistic advances but the diffusion, the broad-spread diffusion of those advances in the form of a high art, but also in the form of a cultural—and this, I think, is important to emphasize—genuine form of cultural entertainment, something that added interest and zest to everyone's life, as well as beauty and truth. In the same sense, 20th century film technology makes the art of visual and narrative metaphor a constant part of our everyday cultural experience.

Remembering Marshall McLuhan's famous hypothesis "The medium is the message," we can immediately recognize that film seems to be the ideal medium—at least in several important ways— for contemporary culture as we've surveyed it, formed an impression of it, in these lectures because of film's capacity for sending mixed messages. We live, in other words, in a complex and ambiguous set of cultural dynamics and film has the capacity for communicating an experience of many meanings at once, of multiple factors and forces because of the flexibility that's built into the very technology of the art form; that flexibility—special effects are just one indication of this—the ways in which the medium itself becomes not only a way of conveying the message but an actual experience of the meaning of the message. Film can express and stimulate a range of imaginative possibilities in ways that are genuinely new. At the same time, however, this highly adaptable medium both registers and contributes to a certain level of confusion of roles between the metaphors of hero and saint; a confusion that's characteristic of contemporary society, a society that's powerfully challenged by cultural forces that, as we have seen, are constantly and powerfully pushing toward totalizing the immediate threat to humanity that threaten the possible death of the human imagination through exposure to violent force.

It only makes sense, in other words, that this highly sensitive and adaptive medium would register the way in which force and, as we've seen, the reality of genuine blunt force trauma to the human imagination throws us off balance, creates confusion so that we wobble; become a little bit tipsy in our balance with regard to the role of the hero and the role of the saint. In a sense, as we survey the testimony of the movies, we see that wobbling, that lack of clarity, that confusion, that question of trying to find our balance again in a genuinely new environment. Film has all of the strengths of the art forms that preceded it; film combines the imagistic richness and depth of texture that the plastic arts possess—painting, sculpture—with the dynamism, the movement of music and dance. Furthermore, film both complements and competes with live drama; the immediacy of live presence that we experience in dramatic theater is rivaled by the virtually unlimited liberty of perspective and effect that is possible with the technologically of film. What you lose in the reality of being in the presence of living human beings is gained by the wizardry of perspective, ways of engaging that presence that the flexibility of digital film offers.

The images of heroes and saints portrayed in different genres of film reflect the complex dynamics of continuity amid change that we have observed at work in 20th century and its culture as a whole. Taken together, the diverse portrayals of hero and saint in film accurately reflect the inescapable ambiguity rooted in the reality of freedom itself that characterizes every aspect of the human search for meaning. Psychoanalyst Ernest Becker, who we will meet again in our next lecture and discuss at much greater length, locates the importance of the role of media in the establishment and maintenance of culture in the following way; he says:

> A working level of narcissism is inseparable from self-esteem, from a basic sense of self-worth. We have learned … that what a man needs most is to feel secure in his self-esteem. But man is not just a blind glob of idling protoplasm, but a creature with a name who lives in a world of symbols and dreams and not merely matter. His sense of self-worth is constituted symbolically, his cherished narcissism feeds on symbols, on an abstract idea of his own worth, an idea composed of sounds, words and images, in the air, in the mind, on paper. And this means that man's natural yearning for organismic activity, the pleasures of incorporation and expansion, can be fed limitlessly in the domain of symbols and so into immortality.

With that rather erudite and scholarly statement of the importance of symbols and the media that conveys symbols, we nonetheless can find an immediate connection to film. I want to use Becker's statement, in other words, to make absolutely clear why it is that for so many of us film is so fascinating, no matter what type of film it is we prefer or what type of film we happen to be exposed to. Friends who have known me for a while say, "Well, if we're stuck for something to put on your tombstone maybe we can go with, 'He would watch anything that moved on a screen.'" And it's true; I had to immediately recognize that that's right. There's something fascinating about the play of life represented through the art and media of the cinema. Becker's point is the reason it's so fascinating, the reason it has such a powerful hold on us, is because the world of symbols—symbols as the carriers of meaning—are our food with regard to what he refers to as our self-esteem, and behind which stands this notion of narcissism. Of course in hearing the word "narcissism" we say, "Whoa, wait a minute. I don't want to be a narcissist; that's not a good thing." But as we'll see in the next lecture, Beckett has a nuanced sense of that notion of narcissism that comes not from its moral connotations—which are negative, certainly—but rather from its psychoanalytic connotations: the notions that narcissism is nothing other than the sheer exhilaration and pleasure of life; the life force that, as he says, wants to constantly take in the world, feed on the world, and convert that food into its own substance and its own vitality.

It's in that sense that we eat up films; we eat up symbolic representation of the playing field, and the boundaries of the playing field—the goals—toward which we're directed. We take pleasure in playing with the different possibilities—two of the main ones being hero and saint—of playing on that field, of moving toward a goal, a satisfaction, that gives completion and wholeness to our experience of living. It is recreational; it recreates our vitality. So, without further ado, let's begin our whirlwind tour of the blazing but also bewildering diversity of images of heroes and saints with which the basic genres of film present us. It is certainly necessarily going to be a whirlwind tour, little more than a brief mention, but just to suggest—and you fill in the blanks—as I said, the dazzling array of different ways in which this extraordinarily flexible artistic medium feeds us images of meaning.

Let's start with the Western: The Western offers perhaps the most specific example of the distinctively American version of heroic identity as articulated in the Myth of the West. Western heroes embody the worldview, well, precisely: of the Greeks. The worldview, the origin—at least in the West—of the idea of heroism; they embody the worldview of harsh, impersonal necessity and the warrior's code: "A man has to do what a man has to do." Iconic examples of this figure of the Western hero as loner, the strong silent type, abound in film. Some of the most classic that come to mind, perhaps maybe first and foremost the film *Shane*: The gunfighter attempting to reform his life, to domesticate himself to the life of the family and to productive labor isn't allowed to do so by the villainous forces of society. He has to strap on his gun again to defend family, to defend community; and then having done so ride off alone into the sunset, up the mountain, leaving behind the call, "Shane! Stay, don't go! We want you here with us." But the hero must go up the mountain to find destiny.

The genre of war films not only explores the traditional image of the warrior-hero in complex ways, but also registers and reinforces the infiltration of total war into contemporary consciousness and conscience. This genre of film provides therefore a useful lens through which to bring the problematic theme of sacrifice into sharper focus. This theme of the heroic soldier him or herself for comrades, for country raises the problem we've seen at the basis of saintly identity from the very beginning. It's the same issue that arises in other genres—books, plays, poems, and operas—but the mass appeal of cinema makes the issue here both more obvious and more pressing, and specifically the difficulty is this confusion conflation of the identities of hero and saint in the popular imagination. So let's dwell on this for just a moment. Strictly speaking, heroes do not sacrifice their own lives; a hero might die in the place of others, but this is a victory, not a sacrifice. This is more than a semantic nicety that we're dealing with here; it's the proper register and effect of two entirely different ways of discovering and articulating the meaning of what's happening in a single event. So it is more than a semantic nicety, this conflation of the worldview of hero and saint; it indicates an unresolved conflict of incommensurable genetic patterns between the two ideal types and the resulting confusion regarding the personal search for meaning. Within the genre of the war film, examples of the heroes who either literally or figuratively sacrificed their own lives for comrades or for their community: Gary Cooper in *Sergeant York*; John Wayne in *Sands of Iwo Jima*; and then in a subgenre very distinctively its own, Vietnam War films such as *Deer Hunter* and *Platoon*. All of these play off of the sense that what the hero does is, in some fundamental sense, both and equally for him and for others.

Another genre: the Biblical epic and classical epics of ancient civilizations. These offers dramatic evidence of the degree to which "In God We Trust" functions as coin of the realm in the 20th century American public cultural values. "In God We Trust," despite freedom of religion, means that we draw fundamental moral and value guidelines from the scriptural tradition of Judeo-Christian-Islamic biblical religion. Whether it's *Ben-Hur*, *The Ten Commandments*, or any of the dozens, literally, of lives of Jesus, these resonate with a culture because no matter what one's religious or non-religious identification, the ethic of love, the saintly identity is so deeply woven into the fabric of our culture that it's a staple part of our diet; it is, as I suggested, the coin of the realm with regard to the economies of culture that we live in. Related to that, Christmas films offer another portrayal of this ambiguous relationship between religion and culture. The iconic film *It's a Wonderful Life*, or *The Bells of St. Mary*, or *Miracle on 34th Street* all demonstrate saintly identity as a normative article of faith in popular culture, and one that functions independently of explicit religious commitments.

The success of some of the fantasy genre of films, such as the first *Star Wars* trilogy by George Lucas and *The Lord of the Rings* trilogy, demonstrates the power of heroic mythic identity as an archetype of human cultural imagination in each of its major elements. Lucas, for example, has explicitly acknowledged the direct influence of Joseph Campbell's groundbreaking book *The Hero with a Thousand Faces* on the development of the central characters in the first *Star Wars* trilogy, especially Luke Skywalker. All the elements of the heroic journey, as Campbell articulates them; all the characteristics of the face that varies infinitely from culture to culture of the hero are contained there in the story of Luke Skywalker. He's called to depart from his domesticated life at home; there immediately arises a dynamic of father/son complication, here Abraham/Isaac; there's a romantic conflict and the role of the unattainable female, unattainable in this case because Leia turns out to be his sister, but that's a dynamic that every hero has to face, the need to struggle to attain an unattainable object, very often in the form of a woman; there's the heroic initiation into the Jedi fraternity; and there's the role of the guide (Obi-Wan Kenobi) as substitute father; all of this we read in Campbell. There's the necessity to defeat monstrous evil, the Death Star; and there's the return home.

Similarly, the *Lord of the Rings* trilogy repeats this same heroic pattern, again offering imaginative freedom and the recreational and entertaining spontaneity of play. It gives us the opportunity to explore metaphorically, artistically the impact of total war. Written by Tolkien out of the European experience, the specifically British experience, of the Second World War, it's obvious that he is playing with, trying to recreate and restructure imaginatively, a sense of meaning about an event that in the living must necessarily register as pure absurdity. It represents, in other words, a mutation of the human condition—this experience of total war—a mutation that has to be dealt with by adaptive behavior. In a sense, the figure of Frodo is a mythic exemplification of the secular saint. That idea might take a little unpacking, but it would certainly be fun to do so.

There are other variations on heroic identity in film: There's the action hero, the detective hero in film noir, the monster as hero (Dracula, Frankenstein). There's the special case of *The Godfather*; one of my own personal favorites in part because it arises out of the Italo-American immigrant experience in the United States which my family participated in, but clearly portrays that same sense of a kind—a very distorted kind, in many ways—of heroism that's based on the idea "a man has to do what a man has to do." In *The Godfather*, it comes across in the words of Sal just before he's taken off to his execution: "Tell Michael it was just business." It's just what has to be done.

Of course the character of Rick Blaine in *Casablanca* is paradigmatic of what at first we say is heroic identity, but I think—plausibly at least—can be seen as embodying the identity of the secular saint, and it forces us to examine what the character tells us about the search for meaning in the popular imagination. At the beginning of the movie, Rick is a kind of disillusioned saint. He has become a loner who makes a living from gambling without taking personal risks himself. Rick has been disappointed in love and has renounced relationship as a source of meaning. At the same time, he's caught up unwillingly in events larger than himself (the war), and in the midst of that context receives a hero's call. Rick discovers the truth about the enduring fidelity of love, and in so doing finds the courage to sacrifice that personal relationship for a higher cause. Rick then ascends to the hero's Valhalla at the end of the film as he strides off to a "beautiful friendship" with Captain Renault. In other words, the film portrays Rick as someone who manages to maintain both of his identities—hero and saint—in a kind of functional balance that avoids surrendering one or the other; and this, my suggestion would be, prefigures the idea of the secular saint as one who is able to support the tension of binocular vision regarding the search for meaning, and therefore perhaps accounts for at least a portion of the film's enduring popularity.

The images of heroes and saints presented on the big screen document both the degree to which the distinct figures of each one have become blended and blurred together in the popular cultural imagination, and the extent to which both of these ideals need continual reaffirmation in the communal consciousness. The question remains whether and when the need for adaptation of these figures will resolve itself into a widespread clarity regarding a new possibility of the ideal type that we've identified as the secular saint.

Lecture Thirty-Four
Ernest Becker—The Denial of Death

Scope:

In this lecture, we consider whether, in the light of the traumatic experience of contemporary culture, we must recognize that this troubled contrast between hero and saint parallels the question of the relationship between life and death. If so, this recognition would require us to reformulate not only both these dichotomies but also our leading question to ask: What is the meaning of life and death taken together, inseparably interconnected as a whole?

Outline

I. We have arrived at a new starting point, a more satisfactory reformulation of our original question: Should the human search for a meaningful life be pursued along the path of the hero or the way of the saint? Does meaning lie in self-fulfillment or is it the gift of love?

    A. The work of Ernest Becker is a basis for asserting that the relationship between the hero and the saint is strictly analogous to the relationship between human death and life.

    B. One specific corollary of this is that the search for meaning is inseparable from the disillusionment born of the recognition of absurdity as an irreducible reality.

    C. Every exclusion or partialization of death from the meaning of human identity is a distortion and loss of its reality.

II. At the basis of Becker's argument in *The Denial of Death* is his contention that the dynamics of heroism, which he claims are universal to human culture, are inseparable from the even more primal universality of terror in the face of death

    A. Becker argues that the heroic self-esteem is a psychological necessity of human identity.

    B. Culture, according to Becker, is to be understood as the outgrowth of the necessity that self-esteem be sustained by recognition won from others.

C. For Becker the so-called life drive expressed as heroism is absolutely correlative to the terror arising from the specifically human self-awareness of the necessity of death.

III. Becker introduces as one of his main contributions the idea of character and identity as what he calls the "vital lie." A sense of identity and self-esteem require the constant repression of the terror of self-knowledge and the certainty of death.

IV. For Becker the recognition of the life/death relationship as one of both incommensurability and complementarity, and ultimately of freedom as the source of all meaning and identity in human existence, leads to what he offers as a kind of distinctly contemporary spirituality, appropriate to the secular saint, which I would characterize as "humiliated hope."

A. For Becker all ideal types including hero and saint are "creative illusion," and the relations among them are irretrievably ambiguous.

B. Becker insists that the only legitimate ground upon which human hope can stand is the "humiliation" of death.

C. Both the humiliation and the hope must be constantly pressed to their limit in order to be realistic.

Suggested Reading:

Becker, *The Birth and Death of Meaning*.

———, *The Denial of Death*.

———, *Escape from Evil*.

Kübler-Ross, *On Death and Dying*.

Questions to Consider:

1. Can you think of other historical figures, beyond those we have discussed here, who have attempted to live the "both/and" life of the secular saint? Do you think they were successful in combining the two paradigms? Why or why not?

2. How might Abraham's willingness to sacrifice Isaac be understood in terms of Becker's concept of the "vital lie"?

Lecture Thirty-Four—Transcript
Ernest Becker—The Denial of Death

As we approach the end of our historical investigation of the ideal figures of hero and saint as paradigms for the human search for meaning, we are now in a position to begin not so much to draw a conclusion, but to recognize that we've arrived at a new starting point, the principal merit of which I would suggest is its timeliness; that is, that it might be in some important sense appropriate for us here and now in the situation in which we find ourselves as individuals and as a society. The starting point at which we've arrived is a more satisfactory reformulation of our original question which, of course, was: Should the human search for a meaningful life be pursued along the path of the hero or the way of the saint? Does life's meaning lie in self-fulfillment or is it the gift of love?

Much of our analysis has been directed toward turning aside as too facile the response that there is really no necessity to choose between the two because somehow they can be combined or integrated without undue difficulty or loss. The weight of historical evidence, at least within the limits of our overview in this course, which of course is only itself a beginning, nonetheless strongly suggests that the dynamics of conversion—as I've tried to characterize them—cannot succeed, but that even if they could it would be at the expense of some part of our humanity. The emergence of the type, the figure, of the secular saint in the 20th century suggests that although there may indeed be something sound in the instinct to say not either/or, but rather both/and—both hero and saint—it's nevertheless, we must acknowledge, quite difficult to imagine what this secular saint would look like in concrete human experience. We have a few examples, yes; but they are by definition extraordinary. But it's even more difficult, bordering disturbingly close to the impossible it would appear, to actually live this ideal. As we said, the few individual examples we've identified—and others that I'm sure with further consideration and exploration you might be able to identify for yourself—genuinely hold out, I think, the realistic hope of imagining our way into the binocular depth of field in our vision of meaning and the balanced sense of responsibility in our human commitments that these figures embody.

In this lecture, we'll consider the work of psychoanalyst Ernest Becker as a basis for asserting that the relationship between the hero and the saint is strictly analogous to—and ultimately derived from—the relationship between human life and death. The search for a meaningful human existence rests on reaching a responsible conviction about the quality of the relationship between the dynamics of life and the dynamics of death, always and everywhere, in human personal identity. One specific corollary of this idea is that the search for meaning is inseparable from the disillusionment born of the recognition of absurdity as an irreducible reality; we've accumulated a variety of testimonies to this reality of the experience of the absurd in human existence. But I think it's important to try to dwell one more time on precisely what not simply the evidence of the idea, the reality of absurdity, is, but the feel of living it.

Let me try to put it this way: The fact of incurable wasting disease is tragic and it awakens human compassion. But the realization that everyday tens of thousands die of diseases that could be prevented or cured is absurd; that millions die of starvation who could be fed, but are not because to do so would require the substantial reduction of the excess wealth of those of us who have more than we need is not regrettable or disturbing, it is absolutely absurd, because it contradicts the experience—intuitive, as well as morally, religiously, socially taught—of a human obligation to all without which humanity can be nothing more than an animal fact. Unless, as Weil said, the life and experience of meaning of each and every human being is somehow or other sacred, than no human life is any more sacred than that of other forms of biological life. I would like to emphasize that in saying this we're not preaching a message of moral or political reform; this recognition, I would suggest, at least as I see it, is purely a matter of that lucidity of intelligence, that perception of reality, that Camus says is possible only on the other side of acceptance that Sisyphus's rock will always tumble wildly to the base of the mountain again, and acceptance of the fact that there is peace and joy only in the space of time it takes to walk back down after the rock to begin the task of pushing it back up again. The absurd, in other words, I would suggest, is absolutely real; at the same time I would also suggest we recognize that it is not the whole of reality.

The consequences that every exclusion or partialization of death from the meaning of human identity is a distortion and loss of its reality; to be out of touch with reality is to become literally unhealthy, that is, literally insane. The implication of this suggestion might point to a certain kind of human spirituality, as we've already suggested, that offers a greater hope for the renewal of humanity in the contemporary historical and cultural context. For example, every hope—whatever its origin—for a happy afterlife, every religious vision of paradise, every Resurrection portrays time as a linear narrative with death as its end point. But what if we imagine life not as a line with a beginning and an end but as an absolute circle with death as its defining center? Then every moment of life already contains death and is in that way after life; what I'm suggesting is that after life could mean that life after death has been taken into account as already and always occurring. Death is the absurd and the absurd is death; nothing more, nothing less. We who live in the absurd world of totalitarian violence, the world of Darfur and of the AIDS epidemic, and of life styles that are sustained by the full faith and credit of financial derivatives whose only resource is speculative, we who live in the midst of absurdity are the living dead; death is at the center of our lives. The only question is what the relation of our lives to the death that is at their center will be. But this is within our freedom to decide; the manner of our dying every day is, as the Stoics said, our principal responsibility; for it alone is within our power.

Returning to Becker: At the basis of Becker's argument in his very important and highly influential book *The Denial of Death* is the contention that the dynamics of heroism, which he claims are universal to human culture, are inseparable from the even more primal universality of terror in the face of death as an absolutely pervasive condition of human experience; all human beings always are in terror of death. Becker argues that the heroic self-esteem that life strives for is a psychological necessity of human identity. Culture, according to Becker, is to be understood as we saw in the last lecture as the outgrowth of the necessity that self-esteem be sustained by recognition won from others. The nature of this recognition is to be understood—as we've discovered in previous lectures—in terms of agon; the struggle of life not merely to survive but to thrive in the competition for scarce resources, both material and cultural. Becker says:

> It doesn't matter whether the cultural hero-system is frankly magical, religious, and primitive or secular, scientific, and civilized. It is still a mythical hero-system in which people serve in order to earn a feeling of primary value, of cosmic specialness, of ultimate usefulness to creation, of unshakeable

meaning. They earn this feeling by carving out a place in nature, by building an edifice that reflects human value: a temple, a cathedral, a totem pole, a skyscraper, a family that spans three generations.

Becker goes on to say that it is self-knowledge of this deepest source of identity and meaning that function as the equivalent—from a very different context—of the gospel saying, "You shall know the truth and the truth shall set you free." In other words, the truth is the truth of self-knowledge; not knowledge of our individual personality, but knowledge of our self as participants in the human condition. And it is that self-knowledge that is freedom; it frees us to recognize reality both internal and external, without which we cannot live. Becker recognizes in this freedom the source of every possible form of transcendence in human experience and imagination; and hence the source of all religions and all cultural institutions without reducing religious faith to an illusion as Freud does. One of the things that is most creative and striking about Becker's treatment is the way in which, in *The Denial of Death*, he puts Freud into dialogue with our old friend Kierkegaard, and it is through this dialogue that Becker tries to achieve the type of stereoscopic vision that we've been aspiring to ourselves in our course.

Becker's point seems to be something like this: Transcendence is never an escape from finitude; it never means fleeing in order to leave limits or death behind. It always signifies the transformation of life drives by passing through the lived experience of those limits, the lived experience of those deaths to become an experience of life having a new meaning—this is the sense of afterlife that we talked about before—after an old meaning that has died. Human beings who are "saved" or "chosen" always remain the same human beings; they always remain human. It's their identity and the meaning of their humanity that's new; the meaning that they have experienced their lives to have.

For Becker, the so-called life drive expressed as heroism is absolutely correlative—can't be separated—from the constant terror arising from the specifically human self-awareness of the necessity of death. Death in this sense—its symbolic sense; in its meaning—is not the same as the biological event of demise (the moment when brain activity stops). Death in the truth of its meaning—true death— is the enactment of finitude and limitation; it's the reality of always coming up short, always coming up against a limit that cannot be surmounted or circumvented. This does not mean that Becker thinks of heroics as caused by death-terror. Neither life nor the heroism of life nor death can ever explain the other away. This is related, I think, to Frankl's idea of the limitations of personal choice; the freedom to choose what sort of response you will have. When you take away liberty—and that happens not just in death, but every day of our lives when we encounter the limits of liberty—we still have, Frankl says, true freedom; the freedom of choice, what that encounter with an insurmountable limitation, what meaning it will have in our life, and how we will respond to it. Without that freedom—the freedom that he identifies as the freedom of conscience—all can be taken away, and one is left with nothing.

Becker, citing the psychologist Maslow among others, strongly argues that objections that a claim for fundamental terror in the face of death can be refuted by empirical evidence that healthy persons are not preoccupied with death is simply a misunderstanding of his point. In other words, what he's trying to suggest is if I say, well, I know lots of sound, solid, integral human beings who don't spend every day of their lives being preoccupied with or terrified death, so Becker must be wrong; Maslow supports Becker in suggesting that it is normalcy, it's an achievement, a hard-won achievement of human character—that is, the human heroic enterprise—and that that enterprise would be like a car without gasoline if it weren't fueled by the constant necessity to say no to death. It is that terror, terror mastered by courage, that is the root of personality, Becker is arguing; and in this we can imagine support coming to him from yet another source. The famous psychoanalyst Carl Jung made what has always struck me as an extremely important point. He says in his writings that human psychological maturity is nothing other than the capacity for conscious suffering; conscious suffering as opposed to unconscious suffering; suffering that is able to face what it knows it must suffer. Whether that be the event of biological demise, whether that be the insurmountable reality of another human being's freedom, whether that be the institutional limits of society, or of the uncrossable boundaries of space and time; the ability to suffer reality consciously is for Jung what it means to be mature, to be healthy, to be normal, to be sane to the degree that any of us are ever normal or sane.

Becker introduces as one of his main contributions to the idea of character and identity this notion that character is what he calls a "vital lie": vital in the sense of it's crucial, we can't live without it; vital in the sense that it is life-giving; and finally that it is a lie. A sense of identity, moral character, and self-esteem necessarily—as I've already suggested—require the constant repression of the terror of self-knowledge and of the certainty of death. Here Becker is quick to point out that as Freud recognized and discovered, the reality of repression is not only a constant in human experience, it's a necessity of human experience. There is a sense in which we're constantly lying to ourselves in that we repress genuine terror at the real fact that our life is constantly threatened in all sorts of ways, both physical and symbolic; we're constantly repressing that and putting that part of reality out of mind so that we can live. It is a lie, but it is a vital lie; so if we don't pass through every day or every hour of life constantly, consciously terrified by the real and immediate presence of death, it's because repression has done its job. But there's a difference between this vital and healthy form of repression and neurotic or even psychotic repression which produces unhealth.

This notion of the vital lie can be understood to include the identity of the saint as well as the hero; sainthood and heroism both require repression. The hero's self-mastery based on self-esteem has to be won from others through agon on the playing fields of culture. The other is the necessary condition of self-transcendence and self-mastery for the hero. And so the guilty debt of the memory of needing the recognition of others as witnesses to and occasions for the hero's self-transcendence can be transformed into saintly gratitude for the gift of life and love received from the other. You see the point here that is in the language of everyday experience the reality that psychoanalysis refers to as transference: We take something that the hero must necessarily repress, dependence on the other; must be repressed for the sake of self-mastery and the experience of integrity of identity. One way of dealing with that repression is the transference of the necessarily killed, the necessarily eliminated other in the transference of that otherness into the object of love and gratitude. Becker makes the point in this way:

> My point is that for man not everything is possible. What is there to choose between religious creatureliness and scientific creatureliness? The most one can achieve is a certain relaxedness, an openness to experience that makes him less of a driven burden on others. ... How does one lean on God and give over everything to Him and still stand on

his own feet as a passionate human being? These are not rhetorical questions, they are real ones that go right to the heart of the problem of "how to be a man"—a problem that no one can satisfactorily advise anyone else on. ... The whole thing is loaded with ambiguity impossible to resolve.

I would add to Becker's statement: It's loaded with ambiguity impossible to resolve because it has its roots in the reality that we identify as freedom.

For Becker, the recognition of the life-death relationship as one of both incommensurability and complementarity—to borrow language from our earlier examination of quantum mechanics—a way of understanding the structure of reality, which I've tried to suggest need not necessarily be limited to the structure of physical reality but might in its own way, properly and metaphorically understood, also be true of inner reality, the dynamics of meaning. This complementarity and incommensurability of the experience of freedom, which is the source of all meaning and identity in human existence, leads to what Becker offers as a kind of distinctly contemporary spirituality, appropriate—I would suggest—to the secular saint, which I would characterize as humiliated hope. For Becker, all ideal types including heroes and saints are, a variation on the notion of the vital lie, creative illusions, and the relations among them are irretrievably ambiguous, as we've seen. This leaves one authentically free and, at the same time, inescapably guilty. Every choice is sin or a lie, but choice is necessity, so all sin must be forgiven. Forgiveness names the humiliated hope at which Becker arrives as his new point of departure. Becker insists that the only legitimate ground upon which human hope can realistically stand is the humiliation of death; the humiliation that death brings. Death is the most basic form of humiliation in the sense that humiliation means being brought back down to earth, to the limitations of time and space, to the finality of finitude. Ironically, Becker seems to identify hope with the freedom always to begin anew after each humiliation or failure; a hope he regards as realistically human. He puts it this way:

> I myself have been fond of using ideas like the developing "spirit" of man and the promise of "new birth," but I don't think I ever meant them to conjure up a new creature; rather, I was thinking more of new birth bringing new adaptations,

new creative solutions to our problems, a new openness in dealing with stale perceptions about reality, new forms of art, music, literature, architecture that would be a continual transformation of reality—but behind it all would be the same *type* of evolutionary creature, making his own peculiar responses to a world that continued to transcend him.

In our remaining two lectures, we'll try to translate this notion of humiliated hope appropriate to the secular saint into a way of going forward in our own search for human meaning.

Lecture Thirty-Five
Terror and Hope in a Planetary Age

Scope:

This penultimate lecture endeavors to put to the test our reformulated question of the meaning of life and death as a whole, as well as the hope which sustains it. The arena for this final agon of questioning and commitment is the contemporary scene of human culture, marked as it is especially by three characteristics, each symptomatic if the evolutionary imperative of adaptation. First, we consider the specter of worldwide terrorism that has supplanted the mushroom cloud as the seal of mutually assured self-destruction. Next we consider the phenomenon referred to as globalization signaling the ambiguity at the heart of capitalism, particularly in its current evolutionary form loosely characterized as "late capitalism," in which economic competition for scarce resources reveals itself to be a more powerful generative force of both societal well being and social conflict than either political or religious dynamics. Finally, we engage the issue of a planetary ecological crisis which credibly threatens to precipitate human culture as whole into the evolutionary catastrophe of species extinction.

Outline

I.   This penultimate lecture is dedicated to testing whether the reformulation of our central question about the search for meaning in life is adequate to the distinct and extreme circumstances of the beginning of the 21st century.

II. Following Becker, we have proposed that human existence is always a question of both life and death and a commitment to search for the meaning of life in death and death in life.

   A. This mysterious reality of existence as a whole therefore must be understood as the origin of freedom of the Fundamental Human Question: Is human existence meaningful or absurd?

B. There must be a real possibility for meaning and for absurdity in both the way of the hero and the path of the saint, and the human experience of living this question must be genuinely and significantly different for each.

C. Therefore, we are proposing reformulating our original question so as to ask: Is it possible—and how is it possible—to live the human search for meaning by following both the path of the hero and the way of the saint, without doing violence to either identity?

III. The first of the totalitarian forces to which humanity is exposed in the 21st century is the crisis of worldwide terrorism.

A. The threat of large-scale global terrorism as we know it today has its roots in the specific trauma of total war.

B. Traditionally, war is the province of the hero; peace is the homeland of the saint.

C. The total war of World War I first defined the cultural space of no-man's-land. No-man's-land now has become everywhere human beings are forlorn as the result of exposure to the extremities of affliction.

D. Is the secular saint adapted for survival in no-man's-land, on the heath with Lear, Vladimir and Estragon, and the Compson family? Such adaptation would require not simply endurance but hope born of the vital desire to be precisely there where affliction lives, not out of compassion, or of obligation, but in the lived experience of the contradiction between the two.

IV. The second crisis of totalitarian force that we are exposed to in the 21st century is globalization.

A. Globalization is a term without a broadly agreed-upon definition, but can be understood as a cluster of interrelated dynamics and issues.

B. The most central impact of globalization may well be its characteristic of ambivalence regarding meaning and values.

C. The secular saint may be considered well-adapted for survival in the absurdity of globalized markets that transcend the regulatory authority of either national sovereignty or moral systems.

V. Finally, the third exposure of contemporary humanity's search for meaning is to the environmental crisis, the progressive degradation of the planet as the organic whole of which humanity is a part.

    A. It is no exaggeration that the planet as a living organism is dangerously diseased and may be headed toward crippling or even lethal conditions.

    B. Only an identity that is not simply prepared to endure death—or even to sacrifice its own life so that others might live—but has the total freedom to embrace death, may be capable of spiritual resurrection of humanity's relationship to the planetary life.

    C. The necessity of this call to learn to embrace death, which Mother Teresa exemplified, is rooted in Becker's unmasking of the source of all human terror and all hope for life in the "organization" of death in human living.

    D. Death is the source of all totalitarian forces in human existence insofar as it is the primal source of terror which is an instinctual and evolutionary necessity before it is psychological as the energy of dread or anxiety that is projected onto objects of fear.

Suggested Reading:

Friedman, *Hot, Flat, and Crowded.*

Gore, *An Inconvenient Truth.*

Questions to Consider:

1. Do you see any positive effects of globalization? How might these affect the role and context of the secular saint?

2. We asked whether the secular saint is adapted for survival in no-man's-land, on the heath with Lear, Vladimir and Estragon, and the Compson family. What would a portrayal of the secular saint in one of these contexts look like? Can you think of any fictional versions of the secular saint?

Lecture Thirty-Five—Transcript
Terror and Hope in a Planetary Age

This penultimate lecture is dedicated to testing whether our reformulation of our central question about the search for meaning in life is adequate to the distinct and extreme circumstances of the beginning of the 21st century. Recall that in our last lecture we suggested that the main achievement and productive outcome of our historical study in this course has been that it puts us in a position to reformulate the leading question of the course—what is the contribution of philosophy and religion to the human search for a meaningful way of life?—into a new, more effective, and timely version of that same basic question. Our reformulation took this form: What is the relationship between the path of the hero and the way of the saint in the human search for meaning in our human existence as a whole, both in our living and our dying. We also tried to construct a very preliminary and experimental prototype model for what this reformulated version of the question might look like and feel like in the experience of living it, because, as Rilke reminded us at the very beginning of our course, the point is to live everything, so that our responsibility is to live the question now, so that perhaps we will, along some distant day, live into an answer. Our prototype model was the metaphor of the secular saint as a kind of evolutionary adaptation of the genetic heritage of both the hero and the saint as it has been passed down through our cultural heritage and has passed into our present cultural environment.

In this lecture, we'll test our reformulated question; take it out for a test drive so to speak, a sort of dry run before venturing out into the fast lane of life. Our test course will be our present situation and our immediately foreseeable future as it might appear in the eyes of the secular saint with particular focus on three especially critical turns in the road—we might call them crisis points; turning points—that realistically call into question the survival of humanity itself in its current cultural species-identity. Those three crises as we'll view them are terrorism, globalization, and environmental degradation. So our test run will involve how the secular saint might respond to these critical turns in the course of the human search for meaning on the journey of cultural evolution. In the last lecture, we asked whether the secular saint is adapted for survival in the "no-man's-land," on the heath with Lear, Vladimir, and Estragon, and the Compson family. What would a portrayal of the secular saint in one of these contexts look like? This is one way of our articulating what our test drive of our prototype model is intended to find out; what we shall see is a particularly challenging course will have to be negotiated to complete that test drive successfully.

You'll recall that, prompted by Becker's distillation in the last lecture of what remains vital in Freud's cultural legacy, we recognized that we needed to reformulate the Fundamental Human Question with which we began—Is human existence meaningful or absurd?—so as to be more precise in one specific way which we took to be decisively important. Following Becker, we've proposed that human existence is always a question of both life and death; always a commitment to search for the meaning of life in death and the meaning of death in life. This mysterious reality of existence as a whole, therefore, must be understood as the origin of freedom in and as the Fundamental Human Question itself: Is human existence meaningful or absurd? It's only when that is a question that there is freedom; wherever there is freedom, reality as a whole is in question. Part of what we now understand here is that for this to be genuinely a question, both possibilities—meaning and absurdity—must be fully real so as for there to be a real choice. There must be, in other words, the real possibility for meaning and for absurdity in both the way of the hero and along the path of the saint, because the question is shared by both; and the human experience of living this question must be genuinely and significantly different for each.

Therefore, we're proposing reformulating our original question so as to ask: Is it possible—and how is it possible—to live the human search for meaning by following both the path of the hero and the way of the saint without doing violence to either identity and with full awareness that such a way of living will require us to be constantly shifting your weight, so to speak, in an effort to keep our balance amid the shifting dynamics of the force field that the tension between these two identities sets up? Sometimes this tension is experienced as being creative; at other times, destructive. At times the effort requires the utmost courage of endurance; at other times we experience it is the joyful exhilaration of play. This process of learning to keep our balance, we have characterized as the necessity to develop individually and societally, spiritualities, ways of keeping our lives in balance and centered through practices of attention; that is, conscious, voluntary, passionate turning of our attention so as to allow ourselves to experience the actual texture of existence, to allow our conscious awareness to taste the fleeting instant of experience on its tongue, to imagine it in its eyes, to listen to it with its ears, to catch the scent of it in its nostrils, and to let our fingertips play across the surface of its skin before we rush into it and rush past it. Our cultures and our traditions offer us vast arrays of spiritual technologies, so to speak; practices that center and sensitize us to the feel of the moment and momentum of experience, the experience of existence as a whole. It is in this inner experience that is what we bring to our encounter with the realities of the world and to our relations with other people. It's this quality of this sensibility that gives the meaning of our lives, whatever form our lives take, and give to those lives distinctive identity.

So this reformulated version of the question would seem to offer the hope of a human way of living that is realistic and timely, specifically in the historical context that's uniquely our own. But as Becker also reminded us, this will always be a humiliated hope, a hope that is never fantastic, exaggerated, or otherworldly, because it is always mindful of the reality of death which brings us back to the earth. Humiliation, being part of the earth (*humus*); we have suggested that the particular character of this humiliated hope will be its promise, because it is a hope, that in the end—the end that we now know means "at its center"—we can find ourselves in the end, at the center, at peace.

Our specific focus of concern regarding the present moment—our cultural present moment—is the threat it poses to human freedom, and its capacity both to take responsibility for its own identity as it chooses, and to sustain the dignity of self-esteem and self-mastery when extremity makes that necessary. We've suggested that out of the trauma of total war in the 20th century a new ideal type of human searcher has begun to emerge—the secular saint—a type of human cultural identity adapted for survival in the forlorn conditions of extreme affliction endemic to sustained exposure to forces of totalitarianism such as those that will forseeably characterize the 21st century even more dramatically than they characterized the 20th.

The first of the totalitarian forces to which humanity will be exposed in the 21st century is the crisis of worldwide terrorism. The threat of large-scale global terrorism as we know it today has its roots in the specific trauma of total war, which as we've seen characterized the last century. Technological advances stimulated by industrialization and the accelerated pace of scientific discovery have produced the realistic threat of "weapons of mass destruction." It's neither an exaggeration nor a sensationalization to assert that we live in an age of terror, more totalitarian in its grip than the Cold War. The metastasis of terrorism into a constant and ubiquitous threat produces a kind of mutation of the form of total war characteristic of the 20th century: world war; a metastasis and a mutation of that into the form that will be characteristic of the 21st century: "the worldwide war on terror." Ironically, this term—the worldwide war on terror—points toward not the hope of peace but rather first and foremost asserts the defeat of war itself by terrorism. No longer do we have nation against nation, but rather terrorism undermines the clarity, the directness, the identifiability of the confrontation of enemy with enemy. Terrorism dissolves violence and diffuses it until no clear line can be drawn. Traditionally, war is the province of the hero; peace is the homeland of the saint. The total war of World War I first defined what we've referred to as the cultural space of no-man's-land. No-man's-land now has become everywhere; human beings are forlorn as a result of constant exposure, total exposure, to the extremities of affliction which the terror of death forces upon consciousness in the form of terrorism.

We want to ask: Is the secular saint adapted for survival in no-man's-land, on the heath with Lear, Vladimir, and Estragon, and the Compson family? Such adaptation would require, as Faulkner said, not simply endurance, but a hope born of the vital desire to be precisely there where affliction lives; not out of compassion alone, nor out of obligation alone, but in the lived experience of the tension between the two, just as Simone Weil embraced death in the sanatorium, fasting in solidarity with French Resistance.

The second crisis of totalitarian force to which we're exposed in the 21st century comes in the form of globalization. Globalization is a term without a broadly agreed-upon definition, but for our purposes it can be functionally understood as a kind of cluster of interrelated dynamics and issues, including some like these: First of all, the emergence of financial markets and multinational corporations that, for the most part, function outside and beyond the authority and control of individual national states and the sovereign laws that those states identify themselves with. Second, digitalization of information allowing for instantaneous transfer of financial and data knowledge capital, creating alternative centers of power in an unstructured environment that resists institutionalization. Third, the heightened accessibility of communication media creating what Guy Debord has referred to as "the society of the spectacle"; where everything is available, everything is open to view, everything and everyone is exposed, and the importance of that exposure comes in the degree to which it can be magnified through media into spectacle: the bigger the appearance, the more real and the more important. This produces a multiplication of cultural theaters, open to decentralized initiatives—anyone has access not simply to the viewing but to the producing as well—aimed at shaping perception to the extent that the line between virtual reality and traditional forms of reality begins to blur.

A fourth characteristic: the accelerated spread of consumer culture across widely diverse local cultures, with the attendant phenomenon of "branding" as a primary source of intercultural identity. The one thing that cultures come to share is the brands by which worldwide commerce identifies itself. An overall decline in the influence of traditional cultural institutions, including political, religious, and military, constitute a fifth characteristic of globalization, and they bring with them a correlative shift toward economic structures as the primary determinants of meaning and value. In other words, no longer is it religion, morality, politics that give basic shape to our experience of social existence, but rather economic forces that reveal themselves to be most fundamental, most basic, and finally most decisive.

The most central impact of globalization as we've outlined it briefly may well be its characteristic of ambivalence in regard to meanings and values: skepticism on the intellectual level, relativism at the level of values. Because it's so powerful a totalitarian dynamic—the very word globalization suggests that it comes to include everything, the whole globe—it consistently presses toward limit-cases wherein its force affects the whole of humanity and of culture in ways that cannot in principle be objectively evaluated according to recognizable and widely accepted norms. Globalization has given new weight to Marxist critiques of capitalism in the wake of the collapse of communism, ironically. The world in which all are alienated from control and responsibility for markets is a world of total alienation; a world that disturbingly closely resembles that of Camus' Sisyphus: The weight of economic reality constantly seems to overcome the efforts of individuals, of nations, and of cultures to sustain its force.

The secular saint may be considered well-adapted for survival in the absurdity and the evil of globalized markets—evil in terms of the suffering that it causes—that transcend the regulatory authority of either national sovereignty or moral systems; an exposure of vulnerable humanity to pure force. As exemplified by King, Gandhi, and others, non-violent resistance may prove the only effective strategy for opposing totalitarianism. The strategy of nonviolent resistance adapted to the economic interplay of globalization may prove the only effective strategy for opposing its totalitarianism. The strategy of non-violent resistance is precisely the mirror image of the strategy of terrorism; that is, using the sheer magnitude of the opponent's force to turn it to one's own advantage. The voluntary embrace of solidarity with the universal poverty of the human condition which we saw was characteristic of Weil, King, Mother Teresa, and others we could readily identify constitutes a source of authentic meaning and value that focuses not on the wealth of nations but on the emptiness of human freedom; its ability not to be anything necessary or determinant; to have real choices precisely because it is not and need not be any thing. That's the poverty that is not only an exposure and a vulnerability, but in this case a resource; this emptiness as the source of humanity's dignity and self-possession. It is a compassion, a community of passionate commitment to the recognition and where possible the alleviation of suffering humanity that affirms the self as free while at the same time upholding the freedom of the other.

Finally, the third exposure of contemporary humanity's search for meaning in the integrity of life and death is to the environmental crisis, the progressive degradation of the planet as the organic whole of which humanity is a part. The current situation would seem to be a movement away from the cycle of life in which generational death is a necessary moment of regeneration, of the perpetuation of the cycle; it's a movement away from this natural, cyclical character of life towards a dynamic that is purely linear, a dynamic that is only one of consumption without regeneration. Again, I don't think it's any exaggeration to say that the planet as a living organism is dangerously diseased and may be headed toward crippling or even lethal conditions. Only a human identity, a way of giving meaning to human existence, meaning even in the face of genuine absurdity; only an identity that is not simply prepared to endure death, or even to sacrifice its own life so that others might live, but one that has the total freedom to embrace death, to make peace with death, may be capable of spiritual resurrection—to use a metaphor—of humanity's relationship to planetary life.

The necessity of this call to learn to embrace death—a peculiar phrase, no doubt; on the other hand we've seen several, I think, role models, heroic, saintly; the first one who comes to mind, of course, is Francis of Assisi. The mark of the stigmata and the way in which Francis envisioned it, and the way Camus perceived it (and for Camus apart from any references to a personal God—this notion of a human being who at the end was ready to lie down in an embrace of loving intimacy with Sister Death. This necessity to learn to embrace death—a learning that clearly requires the simultaneous learning to suffer consciously one's own death throughout life—as Mother Teresa exemplified, is rooted in Becker's unmasking, allowing to become conscious, lifting the necessary repression of the source of all human terror; the source of all human repulsion, resistance, and enmity; and revealing in that same source of terror the source of all hope in life: the hope for life the organization of death into human living. Notice the point of the metaphor there: "organization"; not a structural arrangement but rather becoming organic; allowing ourselves to feel in our nerves and in our blood, and in our consciousness, and in our actions, and in our societies this appropriateness of homeostasis, of maintaining the vitality of the organism through the interplay of the life instinct and the death instinct. Death is the source of all totalitarian forces in human existence insofar as it is the primal source of terror that is an instinctual and evolutionary necessity before it is psychological as an energy of dread or anxiety that's projected outward onto objects of fear.

The terror of death, in other words, is ambivalent in its character. It is the source both of the life driver and the properly identified death drive because it is an awareness of that fundamentally human death that is the experience of the exposure to mystery, as always beginning and as always end. As Mother Teresa's identity reveals, human hope is intimately connected to the direct presence in consciousness of the terror of alienation, withdrawal, separation, refusal of the necessary divine other: mystery for her; mystery in the name of Jesus. The closer she moved to universal love, the more profoundly she experienced the penetration of death into her being. As we saw, her achievements seemed to lie in allowing death the freedom in her experience to become intimate with life. Only such a heightened capacity for freedom will allow humanity to break the addictions to consumption with which it masks and numbs the terror of existence which always includes death; death unreconciled and unforgiven. But the goal here is not to put humanity on a diet, not to declare consumption the enemy; but rather to allow it our need for food, our need to be fed and to feed others, to become a banquet at which all human beings extend hospitality to all others.

Our test drive is concluded, and we'll have to in the next lecture assess what the results have been and where we go from there.

Lecture Thirty-Six
The Secular Saint—Learning to Walk Upright

Scope:

What do heroes and saints have to do with you and me today? Should I commit my time and energy, my trust and hope, and the substance of my relationships to a lifelong search for meaning? There is good and bad news: The bad news is that there is no answer to these questions; the good news is that, for that very reason, because the questions are universal and fundamental to all human beings, we are absolutely free to respond to them as we decide best according to our responsibility to that freedom to be forever, in life and in death, the singular person whose identity is so decided. Heroes and saints are those who have chosen, no matter how they understood the choice and no matter how they went about living it out, to put all their trust and all their hope in seeking the meaning of their freedom and to fulfilling the responsibility which that freedom imposed on them.

The search for a meaningful way of life here, today, for ourselves, has led us to freedom and responsibility for one's own identity as the way of all its paths, and to binocular vision and a practice sense of balance to walk the way of both hero and saint, despite the impossibility of doing so in the hope of being human.

Outline

I. In the last several lectures we have sketched the identity of the secular saint, used that identity to reformulate the leading question of this course, proposed that this renewed experience of the question gives us a new starting point and a humiliated hope.

II. As we review, ask yourself if you recognize yourself in the memory of the journey.

　A. We began with mystery, not as an idea or a proposition but as the experience of the human condition.

　B. Beginning with mystery was a decision; in a sense, all that followed proceeded as it did because of the decision to start with mystery. Mystery is the other of freedom.

C. Freedom and its necessary other, mystery, have this sort of relationship to one another linguistically, because together they articulate what we mean by language.

D. We saw a clear example of this structure of meaning in the opening of the book of Genesis.

E. It was not long before someone realized that this was the result of God speaking: the world is God's creative word; God speaks the language of the world, the language of history.

F. Christianity uses this formulation to identify Jesus as the incarnate word of God, but for our purposes it also expresses a universal human truth.

III. The human search for meaning is embedded in the history of the identities of individual persons and societies.

A. Responsibility is the answer to the human search for meaning, the only possible answer for a question framed as ours is, especially after having traced the evolution of heroes and saints to the present.

B. Our answer in this course—our response, more accurately—has been the figure of the secular saint, which presents a way of articulating the experience of human responsibility as it is happening here and now.

IV. At this point each of us must ask how to go on from here. The question to be decided seems to be something like: Do I see myself in the image of the secular saint, and whether I do or do not, how do I go on from here?

A. My goal has been to help you equip yourself to live the question and commitment of the human search for meaning differently from here onward.

B. Terrorism, globalization, planetary mutation, and other forces will continue to produce traumatic events that will require evolutionary personal and cultural adaptations that effect real changes in humanity as a whole.

C. Our situation is different than it has ever been before because, as a result of historical change, we are more consciously aware of the dynamics of human cultural evolution than previous generations have been, less than future generations will be.

D. But we remain human: We live here and now, in one place and time, which is the culturally situated time and space of our freedom and responsibility.

E. The secular saint does not live human questions in terms of their truth or falsehood, but rather in terms of the way his or her participation in the dialogue shapes that one human identity for which he or she alone is responsible, and for the meaning the one life and death that is given to them within the condition of human existence.

Questions to Consider:

1. How has your understanding of the concept of freedom changed since the beginning of the course? Of mystery? Of metaphor?

2. To repeat a question from the lecture, do you see yourself in the image of the secular saint, and whether you do or do not, how do you go on from here?

Lecture Thirty-Six—Transcript
The Secular Saint—Learning to Walk Upright

In the last several lectures, we've sketched the identity of the secular saint, used that identity to reformulate the leading question of this course, and proposed that this renewed experience of the question of whether or not life has meaning and what that meaning might be gives us a new starting point and a humiliated hope: knowing we need to begin again, and again, always; with a heightened desire to do so, and a deepened commitment to make the question our own by participating in its historical reality here and now. In this final lecture, we will do two more things: First, we pause to recognize that this is a genuine human accomplishment. It's a recognition of the need, the necessity, and the importance of asking the question that takes the form of an act of recollection. We pause to gather the fragments, at least some of them, that had to be left behind in the relentless necessity of time obliging us to move on, to take the next step. Then, a second pause, a moment of reflection, a living instant in the human search for meaning, an experience of the renewed and revitalized question: We've done this together, walked this path, now it ends; what does it mean?

First, an exercise in recollection: Think of it as a picture album of images of heroes and saints and a travel journal of stories told and heard along the way; a sort of cross between *The Canterbury Tales* and the double helix. As we review, I'd urge you to ask yourself if you recognize yourself in the memory of the journey. We began with mystery, not as an idea or a proposition, but as the experience of the human condition itself. Mystery names what must be in human existence: finitude, limit, death, the other. Mystery is the condition that we all as human beings share. Beginning with mystery was a decision; in a sense, everything that followed proceeded as it did because of the decision to start with mystery. Mystery is the "other" of freedom; to start with mystery is also to start with freedom. They belong together as do life and death, meaning and absurdity, heroes and saints.

Later on, we discovered from quantum physics that this kind of relationship has a name: complementarity; or rather this is one of the names that from time to time cultures have given to the structure of meaning itself. Meaning is relationship; meaning is complementarity, correlativity, in the strongest possible sense: "a" is not "a," "a" is not anything except in relation to "b," and the same is true for "b."

Freedom and its necessary other, mystery, have this sort of relationship to one another linguistically, because together they articulate what we mean by language itself. And it is language that makes us human; language names a certain kind of interplay between symbols, between open and closed possibilities. Open and closed possibilities are just like life and death, like yes and no, positive and negative. Together they give us the binocular vision, the depth of field, that's absolutely necessary if we are to approach the question of meaning with any real integrity; with any hope of coming close to a fruitful examination, a pursuit of an answer.

We saw a clear example of this structure of meaning in the opening of the Book of Genesis. In the beginning, God said "Let there be Light"; let the interplay of positive and negative electrons—waves and particles—play itself out and open up the possibilities of the world, and let those possibilities be limited by dividing them up between the wet and the dry possibilities, the bright and the dark, later the male and the female, and still later the good and the evil possibilities. It wasn't long before—once the story had begun this way—someone realized that this was the result of God speaking; the world is God's creative Word, so the story goes. God speaks the language of the world, the language of history. In the beginning was the Word, and the Word was with God, and the Word was God. And then another chapter in the story: and the Word became flesh and dwelt among us. Christianity uses this formulation to identify Jesus as the incarnate word of God, but for our purposes within this course, it also expresses a universal human truth: the truth of metaphor, which is that metaphor is the way truth happens in the history of the relationship between mystery and freedom. Metaphor builds bridges between the two and so expands the possibilities of meaning toward their outermost limits. The Word became flesh, becomes flesh, dwelt among us and dwells among us in the language of the metaphor so that we can know and because we can know, we will seek to know, and we believe that the search will not be in vain; will not be absurd.

That is, will not be only absurd. There will be real resurrection, new, transformed, more authentic life, but only through death. There will be real death, and death is always absurd; there will be real absurdity, and the suffering of absurdity, as Jung said, is the mark of psychological maturity. The capacity for conscious suffering is what makes us human. Death is the experience of conscious suffering; it is the experience of suffering, first and foremost, freedom: suffering the freedom of another, suffering a freedom that is not our own, suffering the freedom that can always say either yes or no, suffering the freedom that is always ambiguous, the freedom that is always divine because it is always altogether other, suffering the freedom that can always say yes, can always say no.

Language, metaphor, and narrative are to what life and death are to human existence. They are the way language enforces some meaning sufficiently so as to be able to bear the full weight of reality. They are the feet on which we walk. The human search for meaning is embedded in the history of the identities of individual persons and societies. It's a history of lives lived in a commitment to questioning which is universal, existential, and dialogical. In this moment of recollection, we recall the words of Rilke with which we began when he reminded us to live the questions now because the purpose is to live everything; by living the questions now there is hope that we might live along some distant day into an answer.

If there is to be an answer to the question for each of us individually and for humanity as a whole, it's to be found in human responsibility; our responsibility to others and our responsibility to ourselves. Responsibility is the answer to the human search for meaning; this I think is one of the things that our historical study has brought forward and enforced, and reinforced most consistently at least in my view, and most successfully. Responsibility is the answer to its own question; the only possible answer for a question framed as ours is, especially after having traced the evolution of heroes and saints up to the present. Our answer in this course—our response, more accurately—has been the figure of the secular saint as a figure of responsibility; a figure that presents a way of articulating the experience of human responsibility as it is happening here and now, which is different than it has happened in the past while still remaining the same.

We've learned certain things from the way the dialogue between heroes and saints has worked out historically. We've learned first that it is a dialogue for which all who participate in it and are affected by it are responsible. It's a dialogue in which all are involved because the dynamic of this dialogue is the dynamic of human existence itself. Our involvement in this universal dialogue of freedom with mystery and of one human being with all other human beings is our absolute responsibility regardless of whether or how we consciously choose to participate in it, because it will decide who we are no matter how we participate in it; whatever the conscious form of our participation and our voluntary attitude toward it might be, it will decide who we are by virtue of our historical enactment of it. It lives in us before we live it.

The reality of this existential decision of identity is what the scriptural religions have traditionally, I think, viewed as Hell and Heaven. Our freedom makes a difference, the way we live our freedom produces a difference that affects and is affected by the whole of reality and the whole history of human freedom as such. Heroes and saints live their existential responsibility differently, and so have distinctly different identities. But the fact that heroic and saintly identities are incommensurable does not mean that they are not complementary, as we've established. One cannot live life the way one faces death, but each of us must do both—live life and face death—continually, because, also as we have seen, death is always at the center of life. Just one example: Recall two faces from our photo album, Sartre and Levinas; a way of living constantly in the face of death; a way of dying that remembers the faces of life.

Once it's become clear that the path of hero and the way of the saint are related to one another primarily as distinct styles of participating in the dialogue that concerns the most fundamental and universal questions of human living that is freedom itself, then our perspective is decisively and permanently changed regarding the role each figure plays in the human search for meaning. One can only walk on one foot at a time, but balance depends on being able to shift one's weight constantly back and forth from one foot to the other in the rhythm that the terrain dictates. Our historical study suggests that we as human beings must try to learn to play both roles—the role of hero and the role of saint—to play them well and to do so as each scene might require. Similarly, our other guiding analogy for the identity of the secular saint, in the same way our field of vision must have a unitary horizon so as to situate objects with realistic depth of field. This continuity of vision requires stereoscopic vision, the autonomic coordination of different perspectives, happening subliminally without having to think about it; it requires this coordination to achieve positional location, what we've referred to as depth of field: the nearness, the farness, the magnitude great or small of that to which we relate ourselves.

As we walk through time, step by step, we stand here or there, but always only in one time and one place. So, too, we're responsible for our life and our death, but differently; and so we struggle to maintain our balance and focus our attention amid the rhythms of experience which have the character of both the personal (the saintly) and the impersonal (the heroic). The secular saint represents a moment of human evolutionary development with regard to the search for meaning and responsibility for identity that loosely replicates that transitional moment of biological evolution when we pass from being quadrupeds to bipeds, and from the monocularity of sensation to the stereoscopy of human perceptions; that is, from instinctive responses to stimuli to seeing things as things in a world through the mediation of language, when we also pass simultaneously to having to deliberately decide what our relationship to those things in the world would be. The human being, the suggestion follows, is an animal that feeds and lives on meanings in a habitat that is charged with values. Survival for the human is specifically the matter of learning to sustain itself in freedom and expand its capacity for responsibility in an environment that is unrelentingly ambiguous, and its ability to adapt itself to thrive on that ambiguity.

Our second movement in this concluding chapter: a moment of reflection before parting. So here we begin to part ways. At this point each of us must ask ourselves how to go on from here. The question to be decided seems to be something like this: Do I see myself in the image of the secular saint, and whether I do or not, how do I go on from here? Our goal has been to equip ourselves to live the question and the commitment of the human search for meaning differently; to participate in it more fully and more effectively from here onward to the degree that each of us can see ourselves in the figure of the secular saint to become more conscious of the ambivalence and ambiguity in the meaning and value structures of our societies and individual lives. The other part of our goal, however, to the degree that any of us should not recognize ourselves fully and truthfully in the image and likeness of the secular saint would be to ask ourselves what alternatives for a coherent reading of personal and cultural identity might emerge from other attempts like this one, but based on different selections of data and following different coordinators for mapping the cultural genome which is our human heredity. None of us can responsibly do less than go on trying to do further for ourselves what we've tried to do together here in these lectures.

As we've seen, terrorism, globalization, planetary mutation, and other forces will continue to produce traumatic events that will require evolutionary personal and cultural adaptations that effect real changes in humanity as a whole. This isn't a pipe dream, the idea of change, both personal and societal. We've traced its dynamics through the extent of human history, and those dynamics will continue. But the question of freedom is how will they continue? Freedom as decisive and responsible participation in mystery is as constant in history as the speed of light is thought (for now) to be constant in our physical universe. Our situation is more different than it has ever been before; as a result of historical change, we are more consciously aware of the dynamics of human cultural evolution than previous generations have been, but at the same time we are less aware—we cannot help but be less aware—than future generations will be. But this is our time, and our place.

Despite the fact that our time and our place are different than it has been previously in the history of humanity, and different than it will be in the future of humanity, we nonetheless remain human. We live as human beings here and now, in one place and time that is the culturally situated and is the cultural time and space of our freedom and responsibility. We do not live in the past nor in the future, but since we live in the present, we live in the time of the question of the hero and saint, and we know this much: that it really is a question whether or not we live for ourselves with the goal of self-fulfillment, or if we live for the other in the hope of love. It always has been a question, and will for human beings always remain so; and that because that question and others like it is more real, more true than any individual's response to it. Living it and participating in it as fully as one can is a way to be human that offers hope, even as it demands the maximum exertion of heart and mind so as not to lose one's balance or close one's eyes to its dizzying ambiguity.

We will not find a secular saint as a partisan in the evolution/intelligent design debate, for example, or on either side of the pro-life/pro-choice debate, on either side of the political aisle or of the religion/atheism divide. Our suggestion has been that the secular saint does not live human questions in terms of their truth or falsehood, but rather in terms of the way his or her participation in the human dialogue shapes that one human identity for which he or she alone is responsible, and for the meaning the one life and death that is given to him or her within the condition of human existence, an existence whose deaths must constantly must be endured with courage and whose loves can always be embraced and cherished if we choose to do so.

So we conclude the course of our journey into the question that the human search for meaning always is; we conclude with a gesture of humiliated hope; the simple gesture of saying that we hope, we trust, we choose to go on questioning, to go on searching in solidarity with one another and with the full conscious awareness that the outcome of that search will decide one thing and one thing only: who each of us, in truth, can say that we are.

Timeline

B.C.E.

c. 1812–1637 (debated)..............Abraham.

c. 1393...Birth of Moses, according to traditional dating of the Torah.

776 ....First recorded Olympic Games.

c. 8th–7th century..........................Homer.

c. 6th century................................Zarathustra.

5th century....................................."Golden Age" of Greek tragedy.

c. 500–400..................................Book of Genesis takes its final form.

c. 470–399...................................Socrates.

431–404.......................................Peloponnesian War.

429–347.......................................Plato.

384–322.......................................Aristotle.

70–19..Virgil.

C.E.

c. 5–67...Paul, originally Saul of Tarsus.

c. 55–135.....................................Epictetus.

70 ....Destruction of the Temple of Jerusalem.

121–180.......................................Marcus Aurelius.

354–430.......................................Saint Augustine of Hippo.

570–632.......................................Mohammed.

800 ....Coronation of Charlemagne as Holy Roman Emperor.

12th century..................................Origins of the Provençal Troubadour movement.

1181–1226...................................Saint Francis of Assisi.

1265–1321...................................Dante Alighieri.

1475–1564	Michelangelo.
1517	Martin Luther's Ninety-five Theses.
1543	Publication of Copernicus's heliocentric theory in *De revolutionibus orbium coelestium libri vi* ("Six Books Concerning the Revolutions of the Heavenly Orbs").
1564–1616	Shakespeare.
1633	Galileo stands trial for heresy and is required to recant his theory that the Earth rotates around the Sun.
1843	Kierkegaard publishes *Fear and Trembling.*
1848	Marx publishes *The Communist Manifesto.*
1859	Darwin publishes *On the Origin of the Species by Means of Natural Selection.*
1872	Nietzsche publishes *The Birth of Tragedy, Out of the Spirit of Music.*
1878–1965	Martin Buber.
1880	Dostoevsky publishes *The Brothers Karamazov.*
1883–1885	Nietzsche publishes *Thus Spoke Zarathustra.*
1897–1962	William Faulkner.
1904–1967	Robert Oppenheimer.
1905–1980	Jean-Paul Sartre.
1905–1997	Viktor Frankl.
1906–1995	Emmanuel Levinas.
1908–1986	Simone de Beauvoir.

1909–1943	Simone Weil.
1910–1997	Mother Teresa.
1913–1960	Albert Camus.
1914–1918	World War I.
1923	Buber publishes *I and Thou*.
1924–1974	Ernest Becker.
1925–1964	Flannery O'Connor.
b. 1928	Elie Wiesel.
1929	Faulkner publishes *The Sound and the Fury*.
1929–1968	Martin Luther King Jr.
1936–1939	Spanish Civil War.
1937	Picasso's *Guernica*.
1939–1945	World War II.
1942	Camus publishes *The Stranger* and *The Myth of Sisyphus*.
1942	*Casablanca*.
1945	Atomic bombs dropped on Nagasaki and Hiroshima.
1946	Frankl publishes *Man's Search for Meaning* (first published in English in 1959).
1946	*It's a Wonderful Life*.
1948	Discovery of the Dead Sea Scrolls.
1949	William Faulkner is awarded the Nobel Prize in Literature.
1953	*Waiting for Godot* first performed.
1957	Albert Camus is awarded the Nobel Prize in Literature.

1958 ....Wiesel publishes *Night* (English translation 1960).

1962 ....Kuhn publishes *The Structure of Scientific Revolutions*.

1964 ....Martin Luther King Jr. is awarded the Nobel Peace Prize; Jean-Paul Sartre is awarded the Nobel Prize in Literature, which he refuses to accept.

1969 ....Samuel Beckett is awarded the Nobel Prize in Literature.

1977 ....*Star Wars*.

1979 ....Mother Teresa is awarded the Nobel Peace Prize.

1986 ....Elie Wiesel is awarded the Nobel Peace Prize.

Glossary

absurd hero: In Camus' thought, this figure is exemplified by Sisyphus, who was condemned eternally to push a boulder up a steep hill only to see it roll to the bottom again. Representing the absurd contradiction between the unlimited and unrelenting human desire to experience the texture of life and to participate in its contests on the one hand, and the necessary contradiction of all such desires by human finitude and death on the other, Sisyphus represents that the futility of his condition can be defeated by lucidity and scorn. In the end, Camus asserts we must regard Sisyphus as happy because he possesses the dignity of maintaining his freedom and can never be defeated in defending it.

affliction: As used by Simone Weil, an intensity of suffering, whether naturally or deliberately caused that does harm not only to personal sensibility but to the universal human desire for good, which is the center and basis for a sense of the dignity and significance of every human life. Because affliction thus humiliates and dehumanizes the sufferer until it annihilates the hope that good will be done, affliction imposes an unconditional obligation on all human beings to do all that is within their power to alleviate it, or failing that, to demonstrate their compassion in a way that makes the sufferer realize that he or she is not alone in his or her affliction.

agape: Christian concept of universal love based on the love of God.

agon: The struggle to get ahead, to win, to excel. A competitive challenge need not necessarily be measured against the performance of others, but can also be measured against the standard of one's own past performance.

alienation: Marx's term for the effect of capitalism, accelerated by the Industrial Revolution, of distorting the relationship between the laborers and the means of production.

amor fati: "Love of fate or destiny" a Stoic conception, adopted by Nietzsche as a characteristic of the Will to Power; understood by Simone Weil to mean obedience to the will of God.

ananke: The impersonal necessity that stands behind and above the will not only of humans but of the immortal gods as well.

arete: The perfect living of one's destiny so as to transcend all others by "doing what can be done by no other." Etymologically formed from the superlative form of the adjective *agathos*, meaning *good*, and *Aristos* meaning *best*.

balance: As used by Simone Weil, this Socratic/Platonic notion expresses her contention that one ought not to seek the good, for it does not exist in the world, but rather to try to counterbalance evil. This is directly related to her ideas of justice as doing no harm and of the universal human obligation to remedy human need, even though it is impossible to fully satisfy this obligation due to the oppression of force which is also universal in the world. For Weil, all a person can hope to do in the world is try to maintain one's balance; consent to the reality of human desire for an unlimited good; and to the reality of the existence of such a good beyond the world of time, space, and human experience.

care of the soul: The way of living advocated and embodied by Socrates as portrayed in Plato's work the *Apology*.

catholicity: "Universality of inclusion." In the narrower sense this refers to what is characteristic of Roman Catholicity, but used more metaphorically, it suggests a vision of some shared aspect of human existence. For example in Flannery O'Connor, material poverty and its extreme—the humiliation which is death—beckon the radical poverty of human existence as an absolute need of the other, and the other as absolute and absolutely inclusive. This universality of need which includes all humanity is the deeper meaning of O'Connor's catholicity.

"church patriotism": A metaphor Simone Weil uses to distinguish a partialization of the whole truth of a basic human need: Humans needed rootedness in a "local" culture with which they are able to identify in concrete experiential ways which are familiar; at the same time, humans need to participate in forms of community which are universal and transcend the strictures of any particular "homeland." The overemphasis of the first is bigotry, the overemphasis of the second is totalitarianism.

citizen-hero: The evolutionary form of the traditional Greek epic and tragic heroic ideal which Plato elaborates in the figure of the philosopher-king presented in the *Republic*, which in turn is based on the portrait of Socrates presented in the *Apology*.

complementarity: A principle of quantum mechanics developed by Bohr and Heisenberg which states that a quantum entity such as an electron may be observed to behave as a wave or as a particle, but never as both simultaneously, although in some sense it exists as both. Thus, any single attempt to measure or observe the system will necessarily be incomplete.

conversion: In general, a significant change in a person's way of life resulting in a new personal identity, often signaled by a change of name. Specifically in the context of this course, conversion is often used metaphorically to refer to the a process of cultural transformation wherein the worldview, meaning and value structures, and idealized role models of a major cultural tradition are incorporated into the identity of an ascendant culture in the expectation that the incorporation can be largely accomplished without significant remainder.

dread (anxiety): As used primarily by Kierkegaard, but echoed in in-depth psychology and, famously in Heidegger, the self-consciousness of human existence as a tension of opposites: physical embodiment and self-consciousness. Situated halfway between the animal, bounded and secured by instinct, and the divine, the symbolic realm of the unlimited capacity for possibility and meaningful relationship.

eudaimonia: The highest level of happiness attainable, the vision of nature, which can be achieved through contemplation.

existentialism: Originally used by Sartre to describe by his work, the term was subsequently applied to various writers including de Beauvoir; Camus, who rejected the label; and, as precursors to existentialism, Kierkegaard and Nietzsche. The term does not encompass a cohesive movement and is difficult to define precisely. Our focus here is on existentialism's insistence to identify human existence in regard to the meaning of one's life.

fatalism: The view that we are powerless to do anything other than what we actually do, that all events are predetermined by some higher power. Augustine rejected this view, instead emphasizing human personal responsibility.

Fundamental Human Question: The question of questioning itself: Is human existence in the midst of the reality of mystery meaningful or absurd? Is there any point to questioning at all if what we are questioning is, in reality, mysterious? Questioning is a decision, a responsibility, a commitment to a way of going on in life, a way of searching for meaning in the midst of mystery. The other possible decision is a refusal, a withholding and withdrawing, the recognition of alienation, of permanent exile, of absurdity.

hajj: The fifth pillar of Islam, the pilgrimage to Mecca at least once in the lifetime of each Muslim, affirming that life is centered on Allah.

hero: In the Greek worldview, the person who recognizes and accepts his fate, *moira*, within the absolute necessity of the divine cosmic order and struggles to fulfill it as completely as possible, thereby achieving excellence, *arete*.

hijra: In 622 Muhammed and his followers emigrated from Mecca to Medina. This journey, the *hijra*, marks the beginning of the Muslim calendar.

historical materialism: Marx's premise that human identity derives from the capacity for labor, that is, the transformation of nature in productive ways.

jihad: To strive or struggle; sometimes referred to as the sixth pillar of Islam because it expresses the need for Muslims to fulfill the mission to spread the Islamic community, primarily but not exclusively by peaceful means.

kenosis: The self-emptying by which God abandons the richness of divinity and takes on "the form of a slave," a willing self-impoverishment so as to share intimately in the poverty and humility of human life.

Knight of Faith: Kierkegaard's characterization of Abraham as an idealized version of the saint. The knight of faith must pass through three stages of self-development: the aesthetic, moral resignation, and faith.

liberty of choice: Refers to the way which we deal with external, circumstantial situations. Like a restaurant menu, every situation constitutes a set of options among which we may choose, excluding other options. Liberty of choice is our capacity to select for ourselves without arbitrary constraint from the options that are or should be available to us. Freedom, on the other hand, has to do with the capacity of each person to decide what his or her identity as a person will be. Freedom, in other words, is freedom of conscience, the ability to choose one's own way. According to Frankl, liberty of choice and freedom constitute a dichotomy equivalent to that of body and soul.

logotherapy: Literally, "meaning-therapy," the type of psychotherapy practiced by Viktor Frankl.

Manichaeism: A religion which originated in 3rd-century Persia and spread widely, centers around the idea of dualism, meaning that the universe is controlled by competing forces of good and evil. In humans the good force of light is represented by the soul and the evil force of darkness by the body. Before converting to Christianity, Augustine followed Manichaeism, and its influence can be seen in his writings.

metaphor: Metaphor is a concrete, particular image, functioning in a definite narrative context, which creates a tension between its specific meaning in its own context and broader possibilities for meaning whose significance reach out beyond the original image into the most fundamental and universal questions of meaning regarding human existence as a whole. Metaphor functions by activating the tensions of opposites that characterize human experience and focusing the energy of these tensions in order to help us understand that experience more fully as a whole.

mimesis: Imitation. Art should imitate life, Aristotle claims, not in the sense of being an accurate copy of the superficial appearances of everyday experience, but rather in the sense of being "true to life," portraying human actions and their consequences in a way that the audience can readily accept as being realistically possible.

moira: Fate, in the sense of individual destiny, both as limit and gift. Etymologically, the word signifies that portion of divine necessity that is dispensed or meted out to an individual human person as uniquely his or her own.

mystery: Mystery names the fundamental experience of all human life in its essential structure of tension between opposite but interrelated possibilities: the experience of a power larger than the human, which resists and limits human understanding and initiative in the world; the experience of finitude, epitomized by death; and the corollary experience of a power that both invites and capacitates a limited but effective transcendence of the boundaries of human existence and the possibilities of becoming at home in the world despite its unremitting enclosure by mystery. Mystery is not a trackless void but a field of force, like gravity, in which a set of navigational coordinates has already become embedded: not north, south, east, and west, but presence, absence, same, and different.

object-loss: Anxiety arising in the early stages of infant life from a pre-conceptual awareness of the child's absolute dependence on the mother, stemming from experiences of loneliness when the mother is absent, frustration when deprived of gratification, irritation at hunger and discomfort, and so on. This anxiety, which if abandoned the instance world would drop away, is viewed as a natural, organic fear of annihilation and death. It is, in fact, the precursor of a cognitive, conceptual idea of death. It is the first trace and register in consciousness of the reality of finitude, limitation, and vulnerability.

Overman or **Superman** (*Übermensch*): Nietzsche's concept of the one who is to come as the future toward which human existence is directed. For Nietzsche the Overman embodies the "Will to Power," and as such, the fulfillment of the human search for meaning.

paradigm shift: According to Thomas Kuhn, these are changes in the broadest horizons of meaning against which specific explanatory theories are profiled. A shift of horizon changes the depth of field in the observer's perspective so that the relation among its objects changes significantly.

philosopher-king: An ideal figure presented in the context of Plato's *Republic* as one who has undergone a long and rigorous educational curriculum designed to educate both body and soul to be fully qualified to rule oneself and to participate with others similarly educated in the rule of society. Plato took the existence of such rulers to be necessary and sufficient condition of progress toward authentic justice in conformity with the reality of the highest good. It can be confidently asserted that the figure of the philosopher-king is the reflection in the medium of Plato's philosophical theory of the lived identity of Socrates as the ideal citizen.

polis: Greek city-state.

saint: Someone who seeks meaning in life primarily by identifying him- or herself through relationships with other persons, human or divine, and specifically with relationships that value some definite idea of Love as the relationship's highest priority.

salat: Prayer, the second pillar of Islam.

Shariah: Islamic law.

sola scriptura: "By scripture alone," a Protestant doctrine asserting that scripture is the sole source of religious truth and authority.

Stoicism: A school of thought dating from the 3rd century B.C.E. that advocated its philosophy as a way of life. Stoicism advocates living one's life in accordance with nature and controlled by virtue. The later Stoic worldview, associated with Epictetus and Marcus Aurelius, emphasized the duty of endurance and resistance to life's suffering.

Sunnah: The religious content of the revelation recorded in the Quran is embodied by the lived example of the Prophet (*sunnah*).

totalitarianism: As used in this course, totalitarianism refers to the full range of cultural crises which concretely reveal the possible impossibility of imagining the future of human existence as a whole. It implies not simply total physical annihilation, but even more terribly the effacement of the meaning and value of human identity as such.

troubadour movement: The troubadour tradition of lyric poetry addresses the theme of courtly love; idolizing romantic attraction between individuals as the most basic and the most transcendent source of meaning in human experience. This movement, which originated in 12th-century Provence, spread throughout Europe.

Will to Power: Nietzsche's conception of the energy that manifests itself in humans as the motivating force behind all actions.

zakat: "Tithe," the third pillar of Islam, literally "purification." It involves thanking Allah both individually and communally by supporting the poor.

Biographical Notes

Abraham: His story in the Old Testament exemplifies the saintly pattern of call or vocation, promise or covenant, and testing or sacrifice. He enters into a covenant with God after God spares his son Isaac, whom Abraham has been willing to sacrifice in a test of his faith. Kierkegaard later terms Abraham a "Knight of Faith."

Aristotle (384–322 B.C.E.): A Macedonian Greek, the most original of Plato's pupils, and in many important ways the most severe of his critics. The difference between their philosophies is significant for understanding the nature of authentic philosophical dialogue, and the tension-filled relationship between philosophical practice and theory. Aristotle's philosophy strives for theoretical knowledge in the idealized form of systematic science. For Plato, Socratic existence is primary and theoretical explanation secondary; for Aristotle the reverse is true.

Saint Augustine (354–430 C.E.): Writer, philosopher, teacher, bishop, and theologian. He is best known for his works *Confessions*, an autobiographical account of his conversion to Christianity; and *City of God*, a philosophical work presenting history as a struggle between the City of God and the City of Man. In a lesser-known work *On the Teacher*, written for his son Adeodatus, Augustine adopts Plato's model of education as the means to correct the evil tendencies born of original sin.

de Beauvoir, Simone (1908–1986): French existentialist writer and philosopher, was closely associated both personally and intellectually with Jean-Paul Sartre. Like Sartre, de Beauvoir asserted that human identity began originally with the act of negation, of saying no to the other, thereby asserting and maintaining itself as free, undetermined by any relationship or meaning except its own, and therefore as capable of taking total responsibility for its own identity. It is from this perspective that de Beauvoir formulates her deconstruction of patriarchy, expressed in her treatise *The Second Sex*.

Becker, Ernest (1924–1974): The son of Jewish Eastern European immigrants, served in the American military during World War II and helped to liberate a Nazi concentration camp. Trained as an anthropologist, his best-known work is the philosophical book *The Denial of Death*, in which, building on the work of Freud and Kierkegaard, he contends that the dynamics of heroism, which he claims are universal to human culture, are inseparable from the even more primal universality of terror in the face of death as an absolutely pervasive condition of human existence. For Becker, sense of identity and self-esteem necessarily require the constant repression of the terror of self-knowledge and the certainty of death.

Beckett, Samuel (1906–1989): Irish writer, most well-known for his play *Waiting for Godot*, in which two men wait fruitlessly for the arrival of an unseen figure named Godot. Other notable works include the plays *Endgame* and *Happy Days* and the trilogy of novels *Molloy*, *Malone Dies*, and *The Unnameable*. Beckett's work is characterized by a sparse and minimalist style; he is sometimes referred to as "the last modernist," paving the way for the postmodern movement. He was a friend and assistant of James Joyce, and associated with Jean-Paul Sartre and Simone de Beauvoir. Beckett was awarded the Nobel Prize in Literature in 1969.

Buber, Martin (1878–1965): Jewish theologian and philosopher, published *Ich und Du* (*I and Thou*), still his best-known work, in 1923. In it, he distinguishes between two fundamental and dichotomous modes of human relationship: the "I-Thou" and the "I-It." In addition to scholarly writings, Buber pursued a revival of religious consciousness among Jews through imaginative retellings of Hasidic tales, an evocative German translation of the Bible, and active leadership of the Zionist movement. He promoted a social-utopian agenda for Zionism, including the establishment of a bi-national Arab and Jewish state as a resolution of the conflict in Palestine.

Camus, Albert (1913–1960): French writer often considered part of the existentialist movement, although he himself rejected that label. Camus was born in Algeria to a French-Algerian settler family. His father died in the Battle of the Marne in 1914. Throughout his life Camus experienced identity conflict, caught between French and Algerian nationalism, Christian and Islamic religious sensibility, and Arab and European cultural identity. As a young man he saw communism as a way of contesting colonial oppression, but he rejected party orthodoxy and moved toward anarchism and joined the resistance during WWII. In 1942, Camus published his first major works: *The Stranger* (*The Outsider*) and *The Myth of Sisyphus*, followed by *The Plague* in 1947 and *The Rebel* in 1951. He was awarded the Nobel Prize for Literature in 1957.

Copernicus, Nicolaus (1473–1543): Polish astronomer, proposed a heliocentric theory of the universe, in which the planets orbit around the Sun. This theory was published in *De revolutionibus orbium coelestium libri vi* ("Six Books Concerning the Revolutions of the Heavenly Orbs") in 1543. Although some of Copernicus's contemporaries—including Martin Luther—found this theory controversial because it seemed to contradict the Bible, it was not officially declared heretical by the Catholic Church. Copernicus's theories greatly influenced later astronomers and mathematicians, such as Kepler and Newton, and he is considered a leading figure of the Scientific Revolution.

Dante Alighieri (1265–1321): Author of the *Divine Comedy*, an Italian poet versed in the troubadour tradition of courtly love. His poem must be understood as a poetic gospel, in the form of a personal testimony to the experience of conversion from sin to the joy of love accomplished through the grace of God incarnated in the flesh-and-blood identity of a human person, Beatrice. His poem is written in the vernacular rather than in Latin, and he is considered to be the father of modern Italian. His life was characterized by political upheaval and ultimately exile from his home in Florence.

Dostoevsky, Fyodor (1821–1881): Russian novelist and philosopher, explored in his writing the psychological and spiritual crisis which confronted the Russian people in the face of sweeping cultural changes. His novels also drew from aspects of his personal life, including epilepsy, extreme financial exigency due to addictive gambling, political exile, imprisonment, bereavement, and professional rejection. His works include *Notes from the Underground, Crime and Punishment, The Gambler, The Idiot, The Possessed*, and *The Brothers Karamazov*. Dostoevsky is widely considered to be a pioneer of the existentialist movement.

Faulkner, William (1897–1962): Influential American writer, known for his portrayal of Southern culture. Many of his works are set in the fictional Yoknapatawpha County, based on his hometown's Lafayette County, Mississippi. His fictional works include the novels *The Sound and the Fury, As I Lay Dying, Light in August, Absalom! Absalom!*, and numerous short stories. He was awarded the Nobel Prize for Literature in 1949.

Saint Francis of Assisi (1181–1226): Born to a wealthy family, experienced a religious calling as a young man and dedicated his life to God through courtly service to the imaginary "Lady Poverty."

In addition to his abject poverty, he is known for his love of animals and nature. He is the founder of the Friars Minor, now known as the Franciscans.

Frankl, Viktor (1905–1997): Austrian psychologist, developed logotherapy, a type of existential psychotherapy based on the concept of the human will to find meaning in existence. His theories were based in part on his experiences as a concentration camp inmate during the Holocaust; he reflects on these experiences in his influential work *Man's Search for Meaning*.

Freud, Sigmund (1856–1939): Austrian founder of psychoanalysis, developed groundbreaking theories of the unconscious mind, including the defense mechanism of repression, the identification of sexual or libidinal desire as the primary motive force in behavior, and his development of the practice of psychoanalytic theory. Freud believed that the psyche could be divided into three parts: the ego, superego, and id. Freud elaborated a worldview and therapeutic technique that owes as much to Greek mythology and tragedy as to contemporary science. Freud, in later works, presents a view of human identity based on the image of the tragic hero who struggles against necessity and death to fulfill his destiny. For Freud, the role of tragic hero was played by the psychic element he termed the ego, which struggled against instinctual drives repressed into the unconscious as a result of civilization's patriarchal authority to limit gratification.

Galilei, Galileo (1564–1642): Mathematician and astronomer who was found guilty in 1633 of heresy for his writings about heliocentrism, which conflicted with scripture. His theories essentially pitted the authority of human sensory and observed experience against the church's doctrinal authority. His work can be understood in the context of the advance of scientific methods which signaled a return to the classical Greek worldview of the hero: a cosmos ruled by the unalterable and indifferent laws of physics.

Hegel, Georg William Friedrich (1770–1831): German philosopher, significantly influenced the work of Marx and others. He developed comprehensive philosophical system to account for the relation of mind and nature, the subject and object of knowledge, and psychology, the state, history, art, religion, and philosophy. Kierkegaard, among others, rejected Hegel's views, particularly his assertion that "the rational is the real and the real is the rational," which for Kierkegaard amounted to a declaration of the superfluity of faith.

Kierkegaard, Søren (1813–1855): Danish philosopher and theologian whose work *Fear and Trembling* portrays Abraham as the "Father of Faith," revealing a disturbing portrait of the dynamics of faith on which saintly identity rests. Kierkegaard, rejecting Hegel's philosophy, saw so-called "Christendom" as a hollow façade of self-righteous justification of a moralistic piety devoid of genuine faith. Kierkegaard insisted that only on the condition of the absolutely paradoxical truth of Christianity, which defied all rational logic, was faith a genuine possibility. Kierkegaard wrote many of his works under pseudonyms, hoping that his readers would interpret them more objectively. His works include *The Concept of Dread*, *Repetition*, and *Either/Or*.

King, Martin Luther, Jr. (1929–1968): Baptist clergyman who became an icon of the civil rights movement; known for his inspiring oratory and his advocacy of nonviolent resistance. King often appealed to scripture and Christian theology to articulate and motivate the cause of the civil rights movement, but also drew on the works of Socrates, emphasizing the dignity of the person as citizen as well as a "child of God." He delivered his best-known speech, "I Have a Dream," in Washington DC in 1963, in which he articulated his vision of an America free from racial prejudice. In 1964, he became the youngest-ever recipient of the Nobel Peace Prize. He was assassinated in 1968 in Memphis, Tennessee.

Levinas, Emmanuel (1905–1995): Russian-born philosopher who lived primarily in France; known for his work on "ethics as first philosophy." Levinas's main legacy for philosophy is a shift of priorities away from knowledge toward ethical responsibility to the other. This is a conversion of philosophy from the "love of wisdom" to the "wisdom of love," as Levinas sees it. His best-known work is *Totality and Infinity*.

Luther, Martin (1483–1546): Leader of the protest which developed into the Protestant Reformation, by virtue of his act of nailing his Ninety-five Theses to the Wittenberg cathedral door. Though initially focused on the Catholic Church's practice of selling indulgences, it became clear that the real point of division was the approach to the covenant's promise between God and man: Does it reside primarily in the heart of the individual who decides through faith to participate, or in the community that is the content of that promise? These questions proved unsettling within the larger religious and cultural religious context of the Enlightenment.

Marcel, Gabriel (1889–1973): French philosopher; often characterized as an existentialist although he himself preferred to be known as a neo-Socratic thinker. He regularly hosted gatherings of philosophers which included Sartre, Levinas, and others. He felt that philosophy should begin with concrete experience rather than with abstract formulations. His works include *Being and Having, The Mystery of Being*, and *The Philosophy of Existentialism.*

Marx, Karl (1818–1883): German political economist, philosopher, and political theorist; widely considered the father of communism. He emphasized the view of history as a history of class struggles. His best-known works are *The Communist Manifesto* and *Das Kapital*. He worked with Engels to develop the doctrine of historical materialism.

Michelangelo (1475–1564): Renaissance sculptor and painter, represents the tension between the humanist and religious traditions. His works, such as *David* and the *Pietà* sculptures, reflect both saintly and heroic influences. He is also known for having painted the ceiling of the Sistine Chapel and its fresco of the Last Judgment.

Nietzsche, Friedrich (1844–1900): German philosopher, wrote numerous influential works including *The Birth of Tragedy, Out of the Spirit of Music, Human, All Too Human, The Gay Science, Thus Spoke Zarathustra*, and *The Will to Power* (compiled posthumously). He is famous for declaring "God is dead," meaning that there are no objective values or universal moral principles. He is also famous for his concept of the *Übermensch* or Overman. His personal life was troubled by health problems, culminating in a battle with mental illness.

O'Connor, Flannery (1925–1964): American novelist and essayist; associated with the Southern Gothic literary tradition. Her works are characterized by grotesque characters and religious themes, particularly the theme of divine grace. She wrote two novels, *Wise Blood* and *The Violent Bear It Away*; and two collections of short stories, *A Good Man Is Hard to Find and Other Stories* and *Everything That Rises Must Converge* (published posthumously in 1965 after her death from lupus).

Oppenheimer, Robert (1904–1967): American physicist; called "the "American Prometheus" for his role in the development of the atomic bomb. Respected for his charismatic leadership of the Manhattan Project, Oppenheimer privately turned to the spiritual poetry of John Donne and to the Bhagavad Gita when contemplating the significance of nuclear weapons. After the war Oppenheimer was a chief advisor to the newly created U.S. Atomic Energy Commission, advocating for international control of atomic energy. His security clearance was revoked during the McCarthy era, due in part to his earlier associations with communists.

Paul of Tarsus (c. 5–64/67 C.E.): Known as Saul before his conversion to Christianity; a leader of the early Christian Church. He emphasized the universality of Christ's message and the importance of Jesus' Resurrection, signifying a new covenant. After traveling through Asia Minor, the Greek Peninsula, and the Eastern Mediterranean as a missionary, he was eventually martyred in Rome.

Plato (429–347 B.C.E.): Greek philosopher; founded the Academy in Athens. He was a student of Socrates and teacher of Aristotle. In the *Apology*, his account of Socrates' trial, Plato establishes the basic characteristics for the figure of the citizen-hero. In addition to the *Apology*, his dialogues include *Phaedo*, the *Symposium*, and the *Republic* (which includes the "Allegory of the Cave"). In the *Republic*, Plato asks the question: Is justice its own reward?

Sartre, Jean-Paul (1905–1980): French writer and philosopher; the most influential figure of the existentialist movement. Sartre's early work prior to and during World War II, especially his novels, like *Nausea*, and plays like *No Exit* and *The Flier*, together with more strictly philosophical works like *The Transcendence of the Ego* and *Being and Nothingness*, present an undeniably bleak and isolated image of human existence characterized by total resistance to everything which is other than the self. Sartre spent nine months as a prisoner of war during World War II. Later, he embraced communism—though never officially joined the communist party—and publicly opposed French rule in Algeria. Sartre was closely associated with the writer Simone de Beauvoir. He was awarded the Nobel Prize in Literature in 1964 but refused it.

Socrates (c. 470–399 B.C.E.): Ancient Greek philosopher; known through Plato's dialogues and other writings. Socrates was convicted and sentenced to death for corruption of youth; his defense is recorded in Plato's *Apology*. For Plato, Socrates embodies a commitment to asking those questions which are both universal and fundamental to all human living. In terms of this course, Socrates' way of life, "care of the soul," embodies the *arete* of the citizen-hero.

Mother Teresa (1910–1997): Born Agnes Gonxha Bojaxhiu to Albanian parents in Skopje, now Macedonia. She joined the Sisters of Loreto at the age of 18 and traveled to India shortly thereafter. She devoted her life to the care of the poorest of the poor, particularly by ministering to the dying. She founded her own order in 1950, the Missionaries of Charity, which has spread across the world. Despite her tireless commitment to her ministry, Mother Teresa wrote of her personal spiritual darkness. Mother Teresa received the Nobel Peace Prize in 1979. She was beatified by the Catholic Church in 2003.

Weil, Simone (1909–1943): French philosopher; born in Paris to a Jewish family. Although her brilliant academic achievements attracted much attention, she pursued a career teaching Greek philosophy in a secondary school for girls in rural France. In the 1930s she was active on the political left, immersing herself in trade union politics and worker education, leaving teaching for a year to experience life as a factory worker. She left teaching again to fight fascism in the Spanish Civil War until an accident forced her to return. She died at age 34 in a sanatorium in Kent, England, of tuberculosis, complicated by her refusal of food to demonstrate solidarity with those in Nazi-occupied France. In the last five years of her life a mystical spiritual perspective unexpectedly opened to her; though she was significantly influenced by the Christian Gospels, she never converted to Christianity. Her writings include *The Need for Roots, Gravity and Grace, Waiting for God, The Iliad or the Poem of Force*, and a number of other essays.

Wiesel, Elie (b. 1928): Jewish writer; deported during World War II along with his family to concentration camps, where his parents and sister were killed. Liberated from Buchenwald in 1945 by Allied troops, he was taken to Paris where he studied at the Sorbonne and worked as a journalist. Wiesel is best-known for his memoir *Night*, a semi-fictional account of his experiences during the Holocaust. He was awarded the Nobel Peace Prize in 1986.

Bibliography

Adams, John. *Doctor Atomic* (DVD). BBC/Opus, 2008. Live performance of the opera *Doctor Atomic* by contemporary American composer John Adams, based on the events surrounding the Trinity test of the atomic bomb and focusing on the extraordinary character of Robert Oppenheimer. Stunning music and masterful staging bring to life the amazing story of the atomic bomb, illuminating the emotional and spiritual aspects of the characters' thoughts and interactions. Also see the Metropolitan Opera *Doctor Atomic* Mini-Site, which provides background information on the history of the Manhattan Project as well as on the work of John Adams. http://www.metoperafamily.org/metopera/news/dr_atomic/index.aspx

Aeschylus. *The Oresteia: Agamemnon, The Libation Bearers, The Eumenides*. Trans. Robert Fagles. New York: Penguin Classics, 1984. This trilogy of plays celebrates the transition from the culture of the blood clan and blood feud to the institutions of civil society governed by the rule of law. It also memorializes the founding by the goddess Athena of the court of the Areopagus, the same court in which Socrates is later condemned to death.

―――. *Prometheus Bound and Other Plays*. Trans. Philip Vellacott. New York: Penguin Classics, 1961. A celebration of heroic identity which Nietzsche identifies in *The Birth of Tragedy* as one of the paradigms of the genius of Greek tragic drama at its height.

Alighieri, Dante. *Divine Comedy: Inferno, Purgatorio, Paradiso*. Trans. Allen Mandelbaum. New York: Bantam (Random House), 1982/1983/1986. This translation of Dante's classic Christian epic is among one of the more approachable for the first-time reader of the poem in English.

―――. *Vita Nuova*. Trans. Mark Musa. New York: Oxford, 1992. Dante's first "published" work, it consists of a collection of poems written over a period of 10 or so years which the author compiled and interwove with an autobiographical commentary shortly after the death of Beatrice, whose story as the object of the author's romantic adoration is recounted here. It concludes with the promise that the author will write, if God allows, an even more worthy memorial to the virtue of his beloved, a promise which is ultimately fulfilled in *The Divine Comedy*.

Armstrong, Karen. *The Great Transformation: The Beginning of Our Religious Traditions*. New York: Anchor Books, 2007. This is an exceptionally insightful and valuable study by an eminent scholar of religion. It traces the simultaneous development during the Axial age (900–300 B.C.E) of a new form of human religious and spiritual sensibility across four distinct cultures: Greek, Hebrew, Chinese, and Indian. It is particularly valuable for indications of how the analysis of the patterns of identity referred to in this course as hero and saint might be extended, with the appropriate qualifications, to non-western cultural traditions.

Augustine, *City of God*. Trans. Henry Bettenson. New York: Penguin Classics, 2003. Generally regarded as the masterwork of Saint Augustine's maturity, it seeks to answer charges that conversion to Christianity was bringing about the imminent demise of the Roman Empire, and at the same time sets forth an idealized model of the relationship of secular society to church authority that would guide European social and political thought for the next 1,000 years.

———.*Confessions*. Trans. Maria Boulding. O.S.B. Hyde Park, New York: New City Press, 1997. This is currently the preferred English translation of Augustine's classic autobiographical account of his early life and education through his conversion to Christianity and the death of his mother, Saint Monica. It is often identified as a turning point in the evolution of the Western conception of human personal identity.

Bakhtin, Mikhail. *Problems of Dostoevsky's Poetics*. Trans. Caryl Emerson. Minneapolis: University of Minnesota Press, 1984. A seminal study of Dostoevsky's "polyphonic" style of novel.

Barrett, William. *Irrational Man: A Study in Existential Philosophy*. New York: Anchor Books, 1962 (1990). The first and still irreplaceable introduction of existentialism to the American audience. The introductory essay (chapters 1–6) is a brilliantly conceived overview of existentialism as a complex and pervasive historical episode. The chapters on the four principal existentialist authors—Kierkegaard, Nietzsche, Heidegger, and Sartre—are helpful previews of their importance.

de Beauvoir, Simone. *The Second Sex*. Trans. H. M. Parshley. New York: Vintage Books, 1989. Widely regarded as providing the theoretical foundations and categories of historical analysis for 20th-century feminism's challenge of patriarchal domination in Western society.

Becker, Ernest. *The Birth and Death of Meaning*. New York: Free Press, 1971. An interdisciplinary study from the perspective of anthropology, sociology, social psychology, and psychoanalysis that lays out the theoretical categories for Becker's later work.

———. *The Denial of Death*. New York: Free Press, 1973. The best-known of Ernest Becker's works and the one for which he won the Pulitzer Prize in 1974 just a year after his death at age 49 of cancer.

———. *Escape from Evil*. New York: Free Press, 1975. Intended by the author to bring to a completion the interpretive project begun in *The Denial of Death*.

Beckett, Samuel. *Endgame*. New York: Grove Press, 1958 (1994). A one-act play by Beckett, featuring the characters Ham, confined to a wheelchair, and his servant Clov, written in a similar minimalist style to his earlier play *Waiting for Godot*.

———. *Waiting for Godot*. New York: Grove Press, 1954 (1982). Arguably Beckett's best-known work and the paradigmatic example of the "theater of the absurd" movement in modern drama.

Ben-Hur. 1959. Along with *The 10 Commandments*, also starring Charlton Heston, this film helped to establish the genre of biblical epic as one of the most widely popular in American cinema.

Bird, Kai, and Martin J. Sherwin. *American Prometheus: The Triumph and Tragedy of Robert J. Oppenheimer*. New York: Vintage International (Random House), 2006. An excellent and very readable biography of Robert Oppenheimer, exploring his role as the "American Prometheus" for the age of the Cold War, and portraying his rise and fall as a heroic figure. The book also presents a fascinating depiction of the culture of the Manhattan Project.

Bodo, Murray. *Tales of St. Francis: Ancient Stories for Contemporary Living*. Cincinnati: St. Anthony Messenger Press, 1992. Modern retellings of some of the stories in *I Foretti* (*The Little Flowers*) of Saint Francis. *The Little Flowers* are a kind of Franciscan gospel, and Bodo is gifted at capturing their enduring spirit and conveying it in contemporary terms. He is the author of many books on Saint Francis and Saint Clare. A very reliable guide.

Brown, Peter R. L. *Augustine of Hippo*. Berkeley: University of California Press, 2000 (rev. ed.). This is generally regarded as the standard biography of Augustine in English.

Brown, Raymond E. *The Churches the Apostles Left Behind.* Mahwah, New Jersey: Paulist Press, 1984. An informative and influential account of the diversity that characterized the early Christian communities as a result of the adoption and adaptation of the preaching missions of individual apostles.

————. *An Introduction to the New Testament.* New York: Doubleday, 1997. Brown is widely recognized as one of the leading authorities in the development of biblical scholarship in the second half of the 20th century. This book constitutes an indispensable introduction to issues of New Testament interpretation.

Calasso, Roberto. *The Marriage of Cadmus and Harmony.* New York: Vintage, 1994. Broadly speaking, this book constitutes a first-rate example of the new light which deconstructive techniques of interpretation can shed upon the traditional cycles of the Greek mythological tradition.

Campbell, Joseph. *The Hero With a Thousand Faces.* Princeton: Princeton University Press, 1948. This book established Campbell's reputation as a preeminent interpreter of comparative mythology. It introduces the concept of the "monomyth" as the pattern of heroic identity which repeats itself with variations across a broad range of world cultures.

Campbell, Joseph (with Bill Moyers). *The Power of Myth.* New York: Doubleday, 1988. This series of interviews, filmed shortly before his death, distills Campbell's key insights regarding the centrality of myth for human identity and culture.

Camus, Albert. *The Camus Notebooks 1935–1942*, New York: Alfred A. Knopf, 1963. A unique perspective on the development of Camus' thought, especially in terms of his encounters with and appreciation of a wide variety of contemporary and historical figures who influenced him.

————. *The Myth of Sisyphus and Other Essays.* Trans. Justin O'Brien. New York: Alfred A. Knopf, 1961. Using the character of Sisyphus, Camus offers his unique interpretation of the absurd as a characterization of the universal human condition, and also as the universal condition of the kind of happiness, which is the authentic fulfillment of human freedom.

————. *The Plague*. Trans. Stuart Gilbert. New York: Vintage International, 1991. In this quasi-allegorical story of an outbreak of plague in the Algerian city of Oran, Camus probes the identity of both hero and saint in the confrontation with the ambivalent certainty of death which constitutes the absurdity of the human condition.

————. *The Stranger*. Trans. Matthew Ward. New York: Vintage International, 1989. Camus' first novel, still widely regarded as most characteristic of his unique identity and place among French writers in the aftermath of World War II.

Casablanca. Warner Brothers, 1942. Consistently one of the top five most influential and popular films of the 20th century. The film's protagonist Rick offers an important perspective on the figure of the secular saint.

Coles, Robert. *Flannery O'Connor's South*. Athens, Georgia: University of Georgia Press, 1993. A fascinating study by the well-known Harvard psychiatrist drawing on his personal experience in the South during the civil rights movement.

————. *Simone Weil: A Modern Pilgrimage*. Woodstock, Vermont: Skylight Paths Publishing, 2001. Highly recommended, balanced and insightful portrayal of a complex human life by a widely respected psychiatrist.

Cook, William R., and Ronald B. Herzman. *The Medieval World View: An Introduction*. New York: Oxford University Press, 2004 (2nd ed.). This book makes a good introduction to the earlier lectures of this course and supplements materials on the Middle Ages not discussed here. Cook and Herzman also have an excellent course on Augustine's *Confessions* available through The Teaching Company.

Cornford, F. M. *Before and After Socrates*. New York: Cambridge University Press, 1932 (1999). A brief overview full of insight into the origins and development of the Greek philosophical tradition by a preeminent commentator and scholar.

————. *From Religion to Philosophy*. Princeton University Press, 1991. Although some of the scholarship has been replaced, the general lines of this analysis of the inseparability of Greek religion and philosophy remain cogent and relevant.

Darwin, Charles. *On the Origin of Species*. 150th Anniversary ed. New York: Signet, 2003. One of the most original and influential books in the history of Western science, it provoked the debate that still rages between intelligent design and evolutionary theory.

Deer Hunter. Universal City Studios, 1978. An important example of the impact of the war in Vietnam on the American genre of war films as a treatment of heroic identity.

Dostoevsky, Fyodor. *The Brothers Karamazov*. Trans. Constance Garnett. London: William Heinemann, 1912 (1951). Dostoyevsky's masterpiece; this is a classic study of the problem of evil and the possibilities of forgiveness portrayed across the members of one family.

————. *The Grand Inquisitor: With Related Chapters from the Brothers Karamazov*. Charles Guignon ed. Indianapolis: Hackett Publishing Co., 1993. Selected chapters from Books 5 and 6, with an insightful and very helpful introduction as well as valuable suggestions for further reading.

Endo, Shusaku. *A Life of Jesus*. Trans. Richard A. Schuchert. Mahwah, New Jersey: Paulist Press, 1978. A unique and particularly insightful reconstruction of the life of Jesus from the perspective of this highly regarded 20th-century Japanese Christian novelist, author of *Silence*.

"Enlightened by Love: The Thought of Simone Weil." David Cayley, Producer. *IDEAS*. CBC Radio One. January 6–10, 2003. An ideal introduction to the thought of Simone Weil in an engaging and highly accessible format. Audio cassette and transcript available at http://www.cbc.ca/ideas/calendar/2003/01_january.html

Epictetus. *Discourses and Selected Writings*. Trans. Robert Dobbin. New York: Penguin Classics, 2008. A more complete elaboration and development of Epictetus's philosophy of human existence.

————. *The Enchiridion*. Trans. Thomas W. Higginson. New York: Macmillan, 1986. An epigrammatic distillation of the spirit of one of the leading proponents of Roman Stoicism.

Esposito, John. *Islam: The Straight Path*. New York: Oxford University Press, 2003 (3rd ed.). An excellent introduction to the religion and its historical development by a leading scholar. Esposito is also the editor of the Oxford *Dictionary* and *History of Islam*, and teacher of a Teaching Company course on Islam.

Faulkner, William. Nobel Prize acceptance speech, 1950. Available at http://nobelprize.org/nobel_prizes/literature/laureates/1949/faulkner-speech.html

Fitzgerald, Sally, ed. *The Habit of Being: Selected Letters of Flannery O'Connor*. New York: Farrar, Straus, and Giroux, 1979 (1999). O'Connor was a prolific letter writer; this collection sheds important light on her life, her insightful analysis of Southern culture, and on many of her individual stories and career as a writer.

Fitzmyer, Joseph A. *The Anchor Yale Bible Commentaries: 31. Acts of the Apostles*. New Haven: Yale University Press, 1998. A leading figure in contemporary biblical scholarship writing in the series widely recognized as one of the most authoritative compendia of Biblical literature available.

Frankl, Viktor. *Man's Search for Meaning*. Trans. Ilse Latch. Boston: Beacon Press, 2006. This best-known of the works of Victor Frankl has been recognized as one of the 10 most influential books of the 20th century in America. Composed of two parts: The first is a memoir of Frankl's experiences and reflections while in a Nazi death camp; the second is a brief overview of logotherapy, Frankl's distinctive style of psychoanalysis.

————. *The Will to Meaning: Foundations and Applications of Logotherapy*. New York: Meridian, 1988. A fuller treatment of the theory and practice of logotherapy.

Viktor Frankl Institute for Logotherapy website. http://www.logotherapyinstitute.org/

Friedman, Thomas L. *Hot, Flat, and Crowded: Why We Need a Green Revolution, and How It Can Renew America*. New York: Farrar, Straus, and Giroux, 2008. An established and highly regarded popular theorist of globalization, this book represents his case for the necessity of a sweeping, coordinated international action to forestall the most serious threats posed by environmental degradation.

Gadamer, Hans-Georg. *Dialogue and Dialectic: Eight Hermeneutical Studies on Plato*. Trans. P. Christopher Smith. New Haven: Yale University Press, 1983. Best known for his magisterial work on hermeneutics, *Truth and Method*, Gadamer's earliest and most sustained philosophical work was on Plato. This collection represents a sample of his insights into individual Platonic dialogues.

Gilbert, Creighton, ed. and trans. *Complete Poems and Selected Letters of Michelangelo*. Princeton: Princeton University Press, 1980. The artist's poems and letters provide fascinating insight into a personal identity as complex and compelling as his artwork.

The Godfather, The Godfather: Part II, and *The Godfather: Part III*. Paramount Pictures, 1972, 1974, 1990.

Gore, Al. *An Inconvenient Truth: The Planetary Emergency of Global Warming and What We Can Do About It*. Emmaus, Pennsylvania: Rodale, 2006. This book was the basis both for a widely distributed film by the same title and for Gore's reception of both the Nobel Peace Prize and an Academy Award in 2007.

Hamilton, Edith, and Huntington Cairns, eds. *The Collected Dialogues of Plato*. Princeton: Princeton University Press, 1961 (1989).

Hartt, Frederick. *Michelangelo* (*Masters of Art*). New York: Abrams, 1984. Hartt is widely regarded as among the foremost commentators on Michelangelo's life and work. This book is a solid introduction.

Hibbard, Howard, and Shirley G. Hibbard. *Michelangelo*. A valuable scholarly and interpretive relation of Michelangelo's life to his works, as well as his poems and letters.

Hollander, Robert. *Dante: A Life in Works*. New Haven: Yale University Press, 2001. A detailed but accessible introduction to Dante's biography in relation to his principal works by a top American scholar and translator.

Homer, *Iliad*. Trans. Robert Fagles. New York: Penguin, 1990. Fagles's translations of Homer's and Virgil's classical epics are widely considered to be among the very best available.

————, *Odyssey*. Trans. Robert Fagles. New York: Penguin, 1996.

Isaacson, Walter. *Einstein: His Life and Universe*. New York: Simon & Schuster, 2008. A highly readable and comprehensive biography of Einstein and introduction to the main lines of relativity theory for the non-specialist.

Islam Online website. http://www.islam-online.net/English/index.shtml

It's a Wonderful Life, 1946. A cinematic classic starring Jimmy Stewart; in some ways, Hollywood's version of Charles Dickens's *A Christmas Carol*.

Kamenka, Eugene, ed. and trans. *The Portable Karl Marx*. New York: Penguin, 1983. This valuable anthology collects Marx's writings (*Das Kapital*, "Critique of Hegel's Philosophy," and others) along with letters, personal documents, chronologies, and other resources.

Karl, Frederick. *William Faulkner: American Writer*. New York: Grove, 1989. An authoritative and illuminating interweaving of Faulkner's life and work by a highly regarded scholar.

Kaufmann, Walter. *Nietzsche: Philosopher, Psychologist, Antichrist*. Princeton: Princeton University Press, 1950 (1974). Sometimes polemical, Kaufmann is the necessary point of reference for discussing Nietzsche in the English-speaking world.

Kierkegaard, Søren. *The Concept of Dread*. Trans. Walter Lowrie. Princeton: Princeton University Press, 1957. A work that influenced 20th-century existentialist thinkers like Heidegger, Sartre, Camus, and Wittgenstein; theologians like Barth, Buber, and Tillich; and a vast array of other 20th-century authors.

———. *Fear and Trembling*. Trans. Walter Lowrie. Princeton: Princeton University Press, 1945 (1952). Lowrie's translations of Kierkegaard have become the standard in English. This work is among Kierkegaard's best-known for its profound and probing treatment of the nature of religious faith through the lens of the account in Genesis of the story of Abraham and Isaac.

King, Jr., Martin Luther. Nobel Prize lecture, 1964. Available at: http://nobelprize.org/nobel_prizes/peace/laureates/1964/king-lecture.html

Kirsch, Jonathan. *King David: The Real Life of the Man Who Ruled Israel*. New York: Ballantine, 2001. David emerges as one of the most humanly complex and distinctly individual figures of the Hebrew Bible.

Kitto, H. D. F. *The Greeks*. Edison, New Jersey: Aldine Transaction, 2007. A traditional academic classic, widely used as an introduction and overview of classical Greek culture.

Kolodiejchuck, Brian, ed. *Mother Teresa: Come Be My Light: The Private Writings of the "Saint of Calcutta."* M.C. New York: Doubleday, 2007. An intelligently edited collection of Mother Teresa's own letters to her most trusted spiritual guides detailing the inner sources of inspiration and of turmoil from which her serene public identity emerged. A necessary source for understanding her complex human identity as well as her worldwide impact.

Kübler-Ross, Elisabeth. *On Death and Dying*. New York: Scribner Classics, 1997. A Swiss-born psychiatrist who moved to the United States in 1958, Kübler-Ross is best known for this influential reflection on the human experience of death as a passage through five identifiable stages.

Kuhn, Thomas S. *The Structure of Scientific Revolutions*. Univ. of Chicago Press, 1962 (1996). The most cited scholarly book of the 20th century. Controversial, but undeniably one of the most influential books on the historical nature of science and its relationship to society.

Levinas, Emmanuel. *Totality and Infinity: An Essay on Exteriority*. Trans. Alphonso Lingis. Boston: Kluwer Academic Publishers, 1991. In this work, originally published in 1961, Levinas lays out his argument for a radical rethinking of the nature of philosophy based on an "ethics of the other," rather than being primarily a pursuit of knowledge.

The Lord of the Rings: Fellowship of the Ring, *The Lord of the Rings: The Two Towers*, and *The Lord of the Rings: The Return of the King*. 2001, 2002, 2003. The popular *Lord of the Rings* trilogy offers an intriguing portrayal of heroism, particularly relevant to this course in its depiction of heroism in the context of total war. Consider the character Frodo as an example of a secular saint.

Lottman, Herbert. *Albert Camus: A Biography*. Berkeley: Gingko Press, 1997. A detailed, thorough, and carefully researched biography of Camus.

Luke, Helen. *Dark Wood to White Rose: Journey and Transformation in Dante's Divine Comedy*. New York: Parabola Press, 1989. Unfortunately prone to go in and out of print, this book is in many ways an ideal introduction to a reflective reading of Dante's *Divine Comedy* as a search for meaning.

Luther, Martin. "The Ninety-Five Theses." Available at Project Wittenberg: http://www.projectwittenberg.org/pub/resources/text/wittenberg/wittenberg-luther.html

———. "On the Freedom of a Christian." Available at Project Wittenberg: http://www.projectwittenberg.org/pub/resources/text/wittenberg/wittenberg-luther.html

———. "An Open Letter to the Christian Nobility." Available at Project Wittenberg: http://www.projectwittenberg.org/pub/resources/text/wittenberg/wittenberg-luther.html

Mahler, Gustav. *Symphony No. 3 in D Minor*. New York Philharmonic (Leonard Bernstein). Deutsche Grammophon, 1989. This masterful work includes a setting of Nietzsche's "Midnight Song" from *Thus Spoke Zarathustra*.

Marcel, Gabriel. *The Philosophy of Existentialism*. Trans. Manya Harari. Seacaucus, NJ: The Citadel Press, 1984. A collection of four essays by this leading French Christian existentialist philosopher; the first two of which argue for mystery as a fundamental philosophical category.

Maslow, A. H. "The Need to Know and the Fear of Knowing." *The Journal of General Psychology*, vol. 68 (1963). Cited by Ernest Becker in *The Denial of Death* as offering important clinical evidence in support of Becker's claim that terror of death is a central and universal formative dynamic in human personal identity.

McCarter, Jr., P. Kyle. *The Anchor Yale Bible Commentaries: 8. I Samuel*. New Haven: Yale University Press, 1995. The Anchor Bible Project is the authoritative resource for the best available contemporary biblical scholarship on individual books of scripture produced in a broadly ecumenical scholarly enterprise.

———. *The Anchor Yale Bible Commentaries: 9. II Samuel*. New Haven: Yale University Press, 1984. The Anchor Bible Project is the authoritative resource for the best available contemporary biblical scholarship on individual books of scripture produced in a broadly ecumenical scholarly enterprise.

McCrae, John. "In Flanders Fields." In *Flanders Fields and Other Poems*. New York: G. P. Putnam's Sons, 1919. (n.b. also available in many poetry anthologies) John McCrae, a surgeon in the Canadian army during World War I, wrote this poem after the death of a friend and fellow soldier in 1915 near Ypres. The poem is often read at war memorial ceremonies.

Meeks, Wayne A. *The First Urban Christians: The Social World of the Apostle Paul*. New Haven: Yale University Press, 1993 (2003). An original and illuminating perspective on the formative influence of Paul in the early development of Christianity by a highly regarded American scholar.

Miles, Siân, ed. *Simone Weil: An Anthology*. New York: Grove Press, 2000.

Mother Teresa Nobel lecture, 1979. Available at: http://nobelprize.org/ nobel_prizes/peace/laureates/1979/teresa-lecture.html

Nasr, Seyyed Hossein. *The Heart of Islam: Enduring Values for Humanity*. New York: HarperOne, 2004. A major scholar's reflections on core spiritual and social values of Islam and their interrelation to other Abrahamic religions.

Needleman, Jacob, and John P. Piazza, Trans. and Ed. *The Essential Marcus Aurelius*. New York: Tarcher/Penguin, 2008. A valuable selection of Marcus Aurelius' philosophical writings together with a helpful introductory essay by Needleman, an important contemporary philosopher in his own right.

Nehamas, Alexander. *Nietzsche: Life as Literature*. Cambridge, Massachusetts: Harvard University Press, 1985. Nehamas is a leading voice among Nietzsche scholars. The book offers a convincing argument for the necessity to view Nietzsche's work as unique and original in both content and style.

Nietzsche, Friedrich. *The Birth of Tragedy*. Trans. Clifton P. Fadiman. New York: Dover, 1995. Nietzsche's first published work; the work of stunning originality and genius, which won for Nietzsche the virulent condemnation of the scholarly establishment in his original academic field of study, classical philology.

———. *The Gay Science*. Trans. Walter Kaufman. New York: Vintage (Random House), 1974. Written in the still formative stage of Nietzsche's development, it offers important insights into the development of leading themes such as power, the proclamation that "God is dead," as well as the theme of eternal recurrence. It also contains much of Nietzsche's own poetry, an indication of the relevance of the title which is based on a then widely known reference to "the art of poetry," with a direct connection back to the Provençal troubadour tradition.

———. *Thus Spoke Zarathustra*. Trans. Graham Parkes. New York: Oxford University Press, 2005. Nietzsche's most emblematic work, loosely based on the historical figure Zoroaster, the Persian religious sage. The figure of Zarathustra as portrayed by Nietzsche in this quasi-mythical, quasi-biblical fiction has his identity primarily as the prophet of a new type of messianic figure, the "one who is to come," the *Übermensch*, or "overman," the culturally evolutionary successor to what Nietzsche regarded as the decadent modern individual.

————. *The Will to Power*. Trans. Walter Kaufmann and R. J. Hollingdale. New York: Vintage, 1968. A highly problematic work published after Nietzsche's death, first by his sister and literary executor, later revised and critically analyzed, the work nonetheless contains important authentic contributions to Nietzsche's mature philosophical viewpoint.

O'Connor, Flannery. *Collected Works*. Library of America/ Penguin Putnam, 1988. The following stories are directly referenced in this course: "Everything That Rises Must Converge," "Revelation," and "A Good Man Is Hard to Find."

————. *Mystery and Manners, Occasional Prose*. Ed. Sally and Robert Fitzgerald. New York: Farrar, Straus and Giroux, 1970. As with her letters, Flannery O'Connor's short essays, speeches, and other occasional prose provide an extraordinarily valuable insight into her personality, her work, her society, as well as to her distinctive imagination and sensibility as a Christian.

Oaklander, L. Nathan. *Existentialist Philosophy: A Introduction*. 2nd ed. Upper Saddle River, NJ: Prentice-Hall, 1992 (1996). This extremely useful anthology brings together excerpts from works by Kierkegaard, Nietzsche, Heidegger, Sartre, Camus, de Beauvoir, and others, along with explanatory text, definitions of key terms, and study questions.

Ormond, John. "The Gift." *Selected Poems*. Bridgend: Poetry Wales, 1987. John Ormond, a Welsh poet and filmmaker, joined the staff of Picture Post in 1945 and, in 1957, began what was to be a distinguished career with BBC Wales as a director and producer of documentary films. Ormond returned to poetry in the mid-'60s, having destroyed much of his early poetry. His first major volume *Requiem and Celebration* was published in 1969, and his reputation was enhanced in 1973 by the appearance of *Definition of a Waterfall* and his inclusion in Penguin Modern Poets. A volume of selected poems was published in 1987.

Otto, Rudolph. *The Idea of the Holy*. New York: Oxford University Press, 1970. A very influential book in 20th-century theology which introduces the idea of holy as numinous, a term which Otto coined based on the Latin term *numen*, meaning "deity, and having the characteristics of being "*fascinans et tremendum*," fascinating and tremendous, in the sense of causing one to tremble.

Owen, Wilfred. "Dulce Et Decorum Est." In *The Collected Poems of Wilfred Owen*, ed. C. Day Lewis. New York: New Directions Books, 1963. (n.b. also available in many poetry anthologies.)

Pelikan, Jaroslav. *Jesus Through the Centuries: His Place in the History of Culture*. New Haven: Yale University Press, 1985 (1999). A valuable contribution to an evolutionary conception of the Christian imagination, by the preeminent 20th-century historian of Christian culture.

Pinsky, Robert. *The Life of David*. New York: Nextbook / Schocken, 2005. The human character of King David is brought to life by Pinsky, the former American poet laureate and highly praised translator of Dante's *Inferno*.

Platoon. Orion, 1986. Like *The Deer Hunter*, another deconstructive adaptation of the American war hero film genre influenced by Vietnam.

Pope, Marvin H. *The Anchor Yale Bible Commentaries: 15. Job*. New Haven: Yale University Press, 1965. The Anchor Bible Project is the authoritative resource for the best available contemporary biblical scholarship on individual books of scripture produced in a broadly ecumenical scholarly enterprise.

Propp, William H. C. *The Anchor Yale Bible Commentaries: 2. Exodus 1-18*. New Haven: Yale University Press, 1999. The Anchor Bible Project is the authoritative resource for the best available contemporary biblical scholarship on individual books of scripture produced in a broadly ecumenical scholarly enterprise.

———. *The Anchor Yale Bible Commentaries: 2A. Exodus 19–40*. New Haven: Yale University Press, 2006. The Anchor Bible Project is the authoritative resource for the best available contemporary biblical scholarship on individual books of scripture produced in a broadly ecumenical scholarly enterprise.

Ratzinger, Cardinal Joseph. *'In the Beginning...': A Catholic Understanding of the Story of Creation and the Fall*. Trans. Boniface Ramsey. Grand Rapids, Michigan: W. B. Eerdmans, 1995. An updating of traditional Catholic interpretation of the first books of Genesis by the influential German theologian who eventually became Pope Benedict XVI.

Renault, Mary. *The King Must Die*. New York: Random House, 1958 (1988 Vintage Books). Mary Renault enjoyed an extraordinary career as an historical novelist specializing in bringing to life the figures of the Greek mythological and cultural tradition. This novel is the first of two based on the myth of Theseus, legendary first king of Athens and conqueror of the Minotaur.

Rilke, Rainer Maria. *Letters to a Young Poet*. Trans. Stephen Mitchell. New York: Vintage, 1986. Small collection of letters written over several years to a young man who sought Rilke's advice on becoming a poet. A rich human reflection on the idea of finding one's "vocation."

Rosen, Stanley. *Plato's Republic: A Study*. New Haven: Yale University Press, 2005. An insightful scholarly commentary on the complex structural and interpretive dynamics of Plato's masterpiece.

Sabatier, Paul. *Life of Saint Francis of Assisi*. New York: Cosimo Press, 2007. A reliable scholarly historical biography of this central Catholic saint.

Sands of Iwo Jima. Republic Pictures, 1949. A classic film of the mainstream American war hero film genre.

Sartre, Jean-Paul. *Existentialism is a Humanism*. Trans. Philip Mairet. London: Methuen, 1948 (1982). First delivered as a popular lecture, this brief essay was intended by Sartre to be a defense of existentialism against the charges of nihilism directed at his thought and the existentialist movement as a whole. While having genuine value as a snapshot of certain key Sartrean themes, it can nonetheless be misleading because of its failure to convey the careful phenomenological bases for Sartre's conception of human existence and freedom worked out so carefully and extensively in his earlier works, *The Transcendence of the Ego*, and the monumental *Being and Nothingness*.

The Searchers. Warner Brothers, 1956. An iconic example of the contribution to the American Western genre by director John Ford, along with such other classics as *Stagecoach*, *Fort Apache*, *She Wore a Yellow Ribbon*, and *The Man Who Shot Liberty Valance*.

Sergeant York, 1941. Directed by Howard Hawks, the film is based on the true story of a country boy who is a conscientious objector who becomes a World War I hero.

Shakespeare, William. *King Lear (Folger Shakespeare Library)*. New York: Washington Square Press, 2004.

———. *Macbeth (Folger Shakespeare Library)*. New York: Washington Square Press, 2003.

Shane, 1953. Arguably, along with *High Noon*, the paradigmatic film representation of the American Western hero.

Shostakovich, Dmitri. *Piano Trio No. 2*. The Borodin Trio. Chandos, 1992. An affecting work which incorporates themes from the Jewish musical tradition in an emotional portrayal of human response to totalitarian force.

―――. *String Quartet no. 8*. Emerson String Quartet. Deutsche Grammaphon, 1999. Dedicated to victims of fascism and totalitarianism, this quartet was composed around the same time that Shostakovich was writing music for a propaganda film about the firebombing of Dresden, and presents a powerful artistic response to the force of violence.

Speiser, E. A. *The Anchor Yale Bible Commentaries: 1. Genesis*. New Haven: Yale University Press, 1963. The Anchor Bible Project is the authoritative resource for the best available contemporary biblical scholarship on individual books of scripture produced in a broadly ecumenical scholarly enterprise.

Star Wars, Star Wars Episode V: The Empire Strikes Back, and *Star Wars Episode VI: The Return of the Jedi*. Lucasfilm Ltd., 1977, 1980, 1983. The popularity of the original *Star Wars* trilogy demonstrates how ubiquitous the hero archetype is in Western culture. Note that George Lucas acknowledged the influence of Joseph Campbell's *The Hero with a Thousand Faces*, and consider how the story of Luke Skywalker fits into that paradigm.

Stockdale, James B. *Courage Under Fire: Testing Epictetus's Doctrines in a Laboratory of Human Behavior*. Stanford: Hoover Institution Press, 1993. An expanded treatment of the material cited below.

―――. "On Epictetus: The Enchiridion," In *Text and Teaching: The search for Human Excellence*. Francis J. Ambrosio and Michael J. Collins, eds. Washington DC: Georgetown University Press, 1991. Former Navy admiral and fighter pilot shot down over Vietnam who spent five years interned in a prisoner of war camp, and later vice presidential candidate in 1992, Stockdale recounts the critical contribution of Stoic philosophy to his ability to survive torture and brainwashing.

Stone, Irving. *The Agony and the Ecstasy: A Biographical Novel of Michelangelo*. New York: Signet (New American Library), 1987.

While not a substitute for a careful biography, an engaging and accurate portrait of Michelangelo's life, personality, and work.

Strauss, Richard. *Also Sprach Zarathustra*. Berliner Philharmoniker (Herbert von Karajan). Deutsche Grammophon, 1996. Widely recognized due to its use in the film *2001: A Space Odyssey*, this symphonic tone poem was inspired by Nietzsche's work .

The Ten Commandments, 1956. Together with *Ben Hur*, also starring Charlton Heston, this film established the genre of biblical epic.

Tillich, Paul. *The Courage to Be*. New Haven: Yale University Press, 2000 (2nd Ed.). Best known and most influential of the works of this 20th-century German-American, Christian existentialist theologian and philosopher.

United States Holocaust Museum website. http://www.ushmm.org/

Washington, James Melvin, ed. *A Testament of Hope: The Essential Writings of Martin Luther King, Jr.* San Francisco: Harper & Row, 1986. This comprehensive anthology collects a wide range of writings of Martin Luther King Jr., including speeches, sermons, and essays, as well as interviews with King. A valuable resource for readers who want to delve deeper than King's more well-known and oft-quoted works.

Weil, Simone. *Gravity and Grace*. London: Routledge and Kegan Paul, 1952. Weil wrote only one complete book during her lifetime, *The Need for Roots*. This collection of religious writings like all of her other books was compiled later from her notebooks, published essays and newspaper articles, and letters.

Weil, Simone. *The Need for Roots: Prelude to a Declaration of Duties Towards Mankind*. New York: Routledge Classics, 2002. A short essay written shortly before Weil's death as a kind of executive summary of *The Need for Roots* for presentation to Charles de Gaulle's government in exile as the basis for the rebuilding of French society after the war.

———. "The Iliad or the Poem of Force." Wallingford, Pennsylvania: Pendle Hill, 1956. Also available in *Simone Weil: An Anthology*, ed. Sian Miles. New York: Grove Press, 2000.) An essay on the Homeric poem written as a reflection on the nature of war as a microcosm of the human condition in its inevitable exposure to the dynamics of force as the basic reality of the material and social world.

————. *Notebooks.* Trans. Arthur Wills. New York: G.P. Putnam's Sons, 1956 Both this work and *Selected Essays* below collect essays and writings by Weil on a variety of topics. However, as both books may be difficult to obtain, the following widely available anthology is recommended for readers seeking an overview of Weil's writings.

————. *Selected Essays 1934–1943.* Trans. Richard Rees. Oxford University Press, 1962. Both this work and *Notebooks* above collect essays and writings by Weil on a variety of topics. However, as both books may be difficult to obtain, the following widely available anthology is recommended for readers seeking an overview of Weil's writings.

————. *On Science, Necessity, and the Love of God.* Trans. Richard Rees. Oxford Univ. Press, 1968. In this collection of essays, Weil explores her ideas about science and faith. Readers interested in Weil's writings on science might also enjoy the more readily available book *Weaving the World: Simone Weil on Science, Mathematics, And Love* by Vance Morgan (University of Notre Dame Press, 2005).

————. *Waiting for God.* Trans. Emma Craufurd. New York: G. P. Putnam's Sons, 1951. Another collection of Weil's letters and essays on religion and spirituality, including the important letter entitled "Spiritual Autobiography," and her essay "Concerning the Our Father."

Wiesel, Elie. *Night.* Trans. Marion Wiesel. New York: Hill and Wang (Farrar, Strauss and Giroux), 2006. The gripping and painfully candid memoir of a Jewish boy interned with his father in the Nazi death camps.

————. Nobel Prize lecture, 1986. Available *at*: http://nobelprize.org/nobel_prizes/peace/laureates/1986/wiesel-lecture.html

Wilber, Ken. *Quantum Questions: Mystical Writings of the World's Great Physicists.* Boston: Shambhala, 2001 (revised ed.). An insightfully edited collection with commentary on the views of a number of leading 20th-century physicists, including Einstein, Pauli, Bohr, and Heisenberg on the underlying unity of the material and spiritual dimensions of reality.

Zilboorg, Gregory. "Fear of Death." *Psychoanalytic Quarterly* 12 (1943), 465–475. Cited by Ernest Becker *in The Denial of Death* as providing important evidence in support of Becker's claim that terror in the face of death is the central formative dynamic in human psychological life.

Notes